OUR PUPILS AND HOW THEY LEARN

TEXTS OF THE LEADERSHIP TRAIN-ING SERIES

1. STANDARD TRAINING SERIES.—A series of studies in the religious needs and capacities of persons of all ages and in ways of dealing with those needs and capacities by means of an effective program of religious education.

2. THE LIVING BOOK SERIES.—A new series of Bible study texts. These texts are of a content nature and are planned to cover the whole Bible.

3. MISSIONS AND SOCIAL STUDIES SERIES.—The texts of this series deal with the interpretation and practical application of the Christian religion.

4. COKESBURY SERIES.—A series of texts designed specifically to meet the needs of the small school by enabling workers to come to a clearer understanding and a more adequate appreciation of their problems and to acquire greater skill in handling them.

OUR PUPILS AND HOW THEY LEARN

An Introduction To
PUPIL STUDY

By
FRANCES C. McLESTER

COKESBURY SERIES
C. A. BOWEN, EDITOR

NASHVILLE, TENN.
COKESBURY PRESS
1930

Printed in the United States of America

In Loving Memory of My Mother
FANNY COLE MCLESTER

FOREWORD

THIS book would be incomplete without an expression of my deep appreciation of the help given to me by my friends as I prepared the manuscript, especially Rev. J. Q. Schisler, Rev. O. L. Simpson, and Miss Lucy Foreman.

F. C. M.

SEPTEMBER, 1930.

CONTENTS

	PAGE
INTRODUCTION	11

CHAPTER I
WHY SHOULD WE STUDY OUR PUPILS? 13

CHAPTER II
WHAT ARE THEY INTERESTED IN? 23

CHAPTER III
WHAT ARE THEY INTERESTED IN? (CONTINUED) .. 42

CHAPTER IV
HOW DO THEY LEARN? 57

CHAPTER V
THEY LEARN MORE THAN ONE THING AT A TIME.. 72

CHAPTER VI
THEY WON'T KEEP STILL 86

CHAPTER VII
WHY ARE THEY SO DIFFERENT? 102

CHAPTER VIII
HOW DO THEY FEEL ABOUT THINGS? 119

CHAPTER IX

They Need Help in Many Ways 135

CHAPTER X

How Do They Grow in Religion? 148

APPENDIX

I. Notes and References 167

II. For Further Reading 174

INTRODUCTION

THE officers and teachers working in the Bethel Sunday School decided to meet one evening each week for three months to talk over the problems that arose in their classes. In the Sunday School Council were the following:

Pastor, Mr. Morris.

Superintendent of the Sunday school, Mr. Brown.

Secretary-Treasurer, Mr. Gordon.

Teachers of the various classes:

Beginner-Primary, Mrs. Chapman; Mrs. Sanders, assistant.

Junior Boys and Girls, Miss Lane, Miss Hopkins.

Intermediate Girls, Mrs. Gordon.

Intermediate Boys, Mr. Newman.

Senior-Young People, Miss Bonner; Mr. Chester, substitute.

Men's Bible Class, Mr. Morris.

Women's Bible Class, Mrs. Ray.

Mr. Newman was the superintendent of the public school in Bethel. He was a college graduate and had taken courses on pupil study, so he was able to lead the other members of the group in their discussions. Miss Bonner had been to normal school a number of summers. She was a public school teacher.

This group was very much like other groups in Sunday schools throughout the country. Perhaps the questions that they asked have been raised by you in your work. The following chapters consist of reports of the meetings of this council. Since the size of this book is limited, the discussions are given in full, but the conclusions that the group reached are indicated. These reports have been published with the hope that they may help you as you work in your own Sunday school.

CHAPTER I

WHY SHOULD WE STUDY OUR PUPILS?

"In our work in the Sunday school all of us run up against various kinds of problems," Mr. Brown said. "So many of the officers and teachers in our school have come to me for advice on different matters that I have decided to make a suggestion to all of you in our Sunday School Council. Suppose we get together once each week to talk over the problems we have with our pupils. Mr. Newman says that he will be willing to lead our discussions. All of us have found him a valuable friend. With the experience that he has had both in day school and in Sunday school, and his training in college, he will be able to help us a great deal as we discuss our pupils."

The Sunday School Council of Bethel Church was having its regular quarterly meeting in the assembly room of the Sunday school. Mr. Brown, the superintendent, had urged all the members to attend, because he wanted to suggest the plan that he had talked over with Mr. Newman some days before. Bethel was the largest Church in a certain town in the South. There were more than a hundred pupils enrolled in the school, and the attendance was usually very good.

"I think that the plan that you have suggested is an excellent one," Miss Bonner said. "In normal school I once had a short course on pupil study, and it has been a great help to me. May we ask questions about things that puzzle us and talk over our troubles?"

"That is exactly what Mr. Brown and I had in mind when we formed this plan," Mr. Newman replied. "When you come up against any problems, you can tell about them in these meetings, and we will see if we can help each other. Of course we shall not be able to take up every kind of problem in the few hours that we will be together, but we can talk about the difficulties that come to us through our failure to understand the people with whom we are working, whether they be children, young people, or adults. When we speak of 'pupils' we usually think of boys and girls, but young people and the men and women in the Bible classes are pupils also. In our discussion perhaps we can learn to understand better why people of every age behave as they do. We shall not have time to settle what type of record books we should use in our classes, or what hymns to select for worship services, or what use we should make of blackboards, or what should be the basis of promotion. These are topics that all of us are interested in, but we must limit our subject. It will probably be best for us to try to find out what makes

14

people act as they do. If we know something about that, we shall be able to solve these other problems more easily."

The members of the Sunday School Council then voted to meet once a week for two or three months, as Mr. Brown had suggested.

"There is one question that I should like to ask all of you right now," Mr. Brown said. "How many of you have thought seriously about why we have a Sunday school?"

"Why, I don't believe I ever stopped to think that through," Mrs. Gordon exclaimed. "I have been a member of a Sunday school all my life, and I have always simply accepted it. But I am sure that it is a good plan to send children to Sunday school in order to prepare them to be good members of the Church."

"I agree with you, Mrs. Gordon," Miss Hopkins said, "but I feel that one of the chief reasons for having Sunday school is to teach the Bible to children, young folks, and adults. I do not think that the older members of the Church should stop coming. There is always a lot they can learn about the Bible, and this is where they are taught."

"Both of you are right, I believe," Miss Bonner said, "but I should say that we have a still better goal in our Sunday school work, one that covers these two reasons and many others. I have been thinking about this very thing since my work in normal school when I had to make out lesson plans and state an aim or purpose for each lesson that I was to teach in the practice school. This year I have been trying to prepare my Sunday school lessons just as carefully as I prepared the lessons that I was to teach in day school. Now, I do not know much about theology, and I cannot say what I want to say in the way that Brother Morris or some other preacher could say it, but I have decided that the aim in my work in the Sunday school is to help the members of my class live as Jesus would have them live."

"After all, that may be the best way of putting it, because it is simple, and yet it covers so much, Miss Bonner," Mr. Morris said. "Of course we want the members of the Sunday school to become good members of the Church and to continue coming to Sunday school after they join the Church. Also we want them to know more and more about the Bible. But we want both of these things because we feel that in this way they will be better able to live together as the children of God. There are other reasons that ministers would give, but I believe that this aim that Miss Bonner suggests would include most of them."

"That is what I should call the *big* aim," Mrs. Chapman

16

remarked. "It is one that we should always have in our minds and that should be the test of all our Sunday school work. However, it is so big that I believe I should feel helpless in trying to carry it out if I did not have what I call *little* aims too, though they are little only in the sense that, taken all together, they make up the big aim that we have been talking about. What I mean is that while we think all the time of leading children and grown people to live more nearly as Jesus would have them live, still there are certain very definite things that we have to work for in turn each Sunday. If you have studied the aims of the group lessons or the closely graded lessons, you know what I am trying to say. For example, one week my aim may be to help my pupils be thoughtful of each other by not crowding each other on the benches or by taking turns in handing out the papers. The next week my aim may be to help them see and really appreciate the beauty of God's world. Later I may be guiding them as they plan to share what they have with those who are less fortunate than they are. Through all this I have in mind the big aim of living together as the children of God, and my aim for each one of these lessons is a part of that main purpose."

"You are right, Mrs. Chapman," Mr. Newman said. "There are what have been called the 'ultimate' or far-off aim and the 'immediate' or present aim. To me, trying to carry on Sunday school work without having a special goal in view is like trying to cook without a recipe, or to plow a field criss-cross, or to weave cloth without deciding on the pattern. We should think through the lesson each Sunday to see just how through it we can help the pupils to live together better. We must never forget, either, that no two pupils are alike and that we must try to meet the needs of each one."

"How are you going to decide what each one needs?" Mr. Chester asked. "I often feel helpless about my own class, because I do not know what I should do for them."

"It seems to me that is just why we have decided to meet here each week for some months and talk things over together," Miss Hopkins put in. "We shall try to learn to know our pupils better, and I think that the first thing to do is to remember how we felt and what we needed and wanted when we were the age of the pupils in our classes. When I was a little girl, my teacher seemed to know how I felt without my telling her, and she was so much interested in me that I would go to her at any time during the week for help or sympathy. She used to tell me what she thought about and what she did when she was a little girl. One day I told her that I wished she was little again so that she could play with me all the time."

"I believe that one good way to learn to know our pupils is to read books on child study and also certain kinds of fiction and stories in magazines," Miss Bonner added. "Stories such as 'Emmy Lou' lead us to 'see into the child's mind.' 'Cambric Tea' and 'Children Are Like That' are two that have helped me a lot. And Booth Tarkington certainly knows boys and girls in their teens; I shall never forget how much I enjoyed 'Seventeen.' It was such a good description of my young brother that I said Mr. Tarkington must have known Malcolm himself. It made me much more patient with Malcolm to have a new understanding of why he often did things that formerly seemed silly to me and provoked me."

"I think that reading even the newspapers helps one understand other folks," Mr. Gordon said. "My father used to talk with us about what he read in the paper, and he helped me learn a good deal about human nature."

"All these things are true," Mrs. Gordon remarked, "but I feel that you are leaving out the most important way of learning to know people, and that is living with and watching the people themselves. Of course sometimes when we watch children we have 'eyes that see not,' as Jesus pointed out. But if we have sympathy for them and really love them we can put ourselves in their place to some extent and can understand them much better. Watching my own children closely has done more for me than anything else. It is my opinion that we can learn from them just about as much as they can learn from us,"

"There is no doubt that we should use all these ways of trying to understand the people with whom we are working," Mr. Newman said, "and I think that Mrs. Gordon's suggestion is an unusually good one. While we are having these discussions I wish all of you would study closely the children and young people and adults in your classes and in your homes and in the stores and wherever else you may see them. Even when you walk down the street you can watch people and try to decide why they behave as they do. For example, on my way to the church this evening I saw a young man and a girl on the street. They had both dressed up in their best clothes, I am sure, and, judging from the way they looked at each other and laughed and talked, they were happy just to be together. Why do you think they acted like that?"

"Well, anyone could tell you that young people like to be together, that they are usually silly, and that they are crazy about pretty dresses and 'sporty suits,'" Mr. Chester replied.

"At least part of what you say is true," Mr. Newman said, "but in the talks that we will have here I hope that we shall be able to see more clearly what people are interested in. We may think that the young folks are silly, but we shall see that the interests that we adults have are built up on those that we had when we were young and that were probably considered silly by our elders. We have come to be what we are through changes that have been taking place gradually through the years. Frequently we are impatient with children or youths because they do not behave as we think they should; but we forget how slowly we ourselves developed, and we judge them by the standards or rules that we have formed after many years of experience. We understand the laws of slow physical growth; we do not expect a boy to grow to the size of a man in a few years. Yet we are inclined to be cross with a child who does not respect the rights of others or who is selfish. Being considerate of others and their rights, being socially minded as some call it, is not something that we are born with, but is something that we acquire. One of the chief opportunities of parents and teachers is to help the young child to develop unselfishness and to learn to respect the rights and properties of others. The failure to do this accounts for a good deal of the stealing and crookedness that is written up in large type in the newspapers."

"Helping children to be thoughtful of others is certainly a part of our big aim of leading them to live together as the children of God," Miss Hopkins said. "All of us agree with you in that. I have that purpose in the back of my mind, but I confess that I am hoping our discussions will help me in very practical ways. For instance, this is my biggest problem at present: why do the boys and girls in my class pay so little attention to what I say to them on Sunday, and seem not to be interested in the lessons I am trying to teach them? They cut up so much that I am puzzled as to what to do with them."

"We shall not have time to talk any longer to-night," Mr. Brown broke in. "Perhaps Mr. Newman will be willing for you to bring up that question a week from to-night."

"Yes," Mr. Newman agreed, "I believe it will be a fine plan to try to find out first of all what people are really interested in. Suppose we think about that between now and next Wednesday evening."

CHAPTER II

WHAT ARE THEY INTERESTED IN?

"I AM glad that we will talk to-night about the problem that I brought up at our meeting of the Sunday School Council last week," said Miss Hopkins. "My boys were worse than usual last Sunday. They threw paper wads and whispered and paid no attention to what I was trying to tell them. I can't get them interested in the lessons, no matter how hard I try. They seem to be interested chiefly in seeing which one can be the leader in misbehaving."

"I do not suppose there have ever been many Sunday school teachers who were not puzzled by this difficulty, whether in big schools or little, in city or in town or in country," Mr. Newman said. "Perhaps we may be able to understand better the things that our pupils are interested in if we try to find out what we are interested in ourselves. To-night I brought with me some magazines— the *Saturday Evening Post*, the *Farm Journal, Better Homes and Gardens,* and the *Woman's Home Companion*. I want all of you to look through the advertisements to see what pictures interest you most. Select the three that you like best and be ready to tell the rest of us why you selected them."

23

They spent a few minutes looking through the magazines, and then Mr. Newman called for a report. "Suppose you start, Miss Hopkins," he said.

"I like this one of the two boys with their dog," Miss Hopkins said. "It reminds me of the boys in my class, and I do love them even though they worry me half to death at times. Then I selected this one of a woman in a pretty dress because I am planning to make a dress myself, and this one is a good style. For the third one I took this one of a train going at full speed. I am always planning the trips that I wish I could take."

"What did you select, Mr. Gordon?" Mr. Newman asked.

"Well, I am so much interested in cars, now that I am planning to buy one, that I have two ads showing them— a sport model and a touring car big enough for all the family. Then I like this one of a modern dairy; I need a new cow barn myself, and I wish that I could afford one like the kind pictured here."

"Tell us about yours, Mrs. Gordon."

"When I found this one I showed it to my husband and told him that he should have selected it himself. It is a page showing three desserts that look delicious. I suppose that I like to cook good things just as much as Mr. Gordon likes eating them, however. My next picture is of a Hoover cleaner, because if I had one it would mean that I should not have to sweep the floors. For the third I selected this one of young people playing tennis because I like young folks so much."

"What pictures did you choose, Miss Bonner?"

"I like this one of a woman working in her flower garden, this one of a fine-looking woman who 'earns a big salary,' and this one of a box of candy. I naturally like flowers and candy, and the other picture appealed to me because I am trying to save money so that I shall be independent when I am an old lady, and I find it hard to do so on my present salary."

"I like this one of a baby trying to put on his shoe, and this one of a beautiful dog, and this one of a radio," Mrs. Chapman volunteered. "And there are others of food and lovely homes and fine-looking cars that I might have chosen if you had not told us to select only three."

"Perhaps these will be enough to help us to understand what folks like," said Mr. Newman. "These dishes of food actually make one's mouth water. Satisfying hunger is one of the chief and strongest desires that all of us have. You know how a person who has had typhoid fever will beg for food even against the doctor's strict orders. In China, where there are such terrible famines, the people become like savages when they are crazed with hunger. We are fortunate because we do not really suffer for lack of food; we usually get it when we need it. The

25

desire for food is one of the first things that the baby will try to make plain. He cannot tell you what he wants, but his loud cries leave his mother in no doubt. The little boy who takes the cookies from the pantry has the same urge for food, and he sometimes forgets even to stop to ask for something to eat. We adults have learned to be more or less polite about our hunger, but you know how cross you are when your dinner is late or when you have to go on a diet."

"Well," said Mrs. Gordon, "I understand better now why Jimmy keeps the tea cake jar empty. He used to eat no more than his sister did; but now that he is twelve, I can't keep enough tea cakes, bread, and preserves on hand. But there is another thing about Jimmy that puzzles me: why does he keep such a queer collection of things in his pockets? He must be interested in everything under the sun!"

"Curiosity and the desire to own things are two very strong urges we all have," Mr. Newman answered. "The little child takes a clock or toy to pieces, the boy wants to see how many different things he can do with his hammer, Edison works on a new invention—all of them are discovering things and seeing what they can do with them. Jimmy is curious about the things he has collected, and he will look them over and find out how he can use them. Also he wants to own things, just as the rest of

26

us do. He has only a few things that he can call his own and can do with exactly as he likes, and he wants others. We want things of our own—cars or houses or pets or modern tractors or gardens or grocery stores or new clothes or a world of other things, according to our age and what we already have, and what our friends have, and so forth."

"Well, I already have a car, but I want a new one," Mr. Gordon said. "My old car certainly does look rusty now that my neighbor has a new model, though I was fairly well satisfied with mine until the new ones came out."

"We not only want to own things," Mr. Newman remarked, "but we want to have our friends and even people whom we do not know admire whatever it is that we have. Occasionally there is a miser who loves money for its own sake and does not want anyone else to know how much he has, but to most of us one of the best parts of owning things is having a chance to show them to our friends. If we are frank, we will confess that we rather enjoy having people praise our new cars, the vegetables we raise, our delicious cakes, our intelligence, our ability to throw a ball, our good looks, our best furniture. Whatever we have, we are glad that our friends know about it. This makes us feel important; and the more other people praise our possessions, the more important we feel. Unless it

27

is carried too far, it is a quite natural feeling and nothing to be ashamed of. We certainly ought to recognize this desire when we are working with other people."

"The desire to show off and to attract the attention of others must have been the reason for my wanting my friends to see my new car," said Mrs. Sanders with a laugh. "It is a relief to me to know that other folks feel the same way about their possessions. Is that why little children show off their new dresses and shoes and their pets and even useless little things that they may have picked up?"

"Yes," Mr. Newman answered, "and the longing to feel important makes them tell their admiring playmates how fast their big brothers can drive and how tall their fathers are and how well their mothers can cook. All of us, big and little, show this same desire to attract attention and have people think well of our families and ourselves. That is why we men and women do not want to wear old-fashioned clothes, why we want the latest model in cars, why we always have a bigger tale or a funnier story that we must tell, and why we want to catch the biggest fish or win the prize in a game."

"Is this same longing for attention shown by the boys and girls of eighteen and twenty when they spend so much time primping?" asked Mr. Chester.

"Yes, and it is not limited to those years, as most of

28

us might admit unwillingly," said Mr. Newman. "It is natural for people to be interested in each other, and with young people this interest is very powerful. They are eager to gain the attention of anyone, but especially of those of their own age. It is one of the laws of nature that boys — —and girls, too—are interested in the opposite sex. Sometimes this interest is shown early, and sometimes it is a bit delayed, but they will have it sooner or later unless they are 'queer.' They would rather have their sweethearts admire them than anyone else. Often they do things that we think are silly when they are trying to attract attention and shine before all eyes, particularly one pair. Besides, if we were in the place of the young people we should not think that these things were ridiculous. We forget just how foolish we were at that age, but I dare say our parents often laughed at us behind our backs."

"I suppose so," said Mr. Gordon, "and I believe that I can be more patient with Thomas hereafter. Some years ago we were distressed about how careless he was of his clothes, and we used to tell him that the neighbors would think he was a tramp. Now he spends so much time pressing his suit, fixing his tie, and combing his hair that he is always late to meals or to his engagements. I know that he usually takes such pains to look well because he is fond of Jane and wants her to be pleased with his appearance. I confess that I used to be that way myself when I was trying to make Betty like me. Do you remember that gray suit of mine, Mrs. Gordon?"

"I believe that gray suit was the one thing that finally made me decide to say 'yes' to you," laughed Mrs. Gordon. "You were so much handsomer than the other boys when you wore it. And Thomas is just like you. Whenever anyone says anything nice about him he tells Jane about it. I've been rather provoked with him at times when he would not pay any attention to what I said, but was very much concerned about what she and the other young people in his crowd might say about him."

"Thomas would be pleased to have us think that he is well-nigh perfect, just as Jane thinks he is; but if it is a choice between us older folk and his own crowd, he would probably not hesitate as to whose opinion he would prefer," remarked Mr. Newman. "The desire to stand well with the people with whom one goes is very strong. We know that is true even about ourselves with our missionary society and our club and our neighbors. We want to look well and to behave just as our friends think we should. We like to be stylish, and to have a good-looking car, and to have people admire us for our success in whatever we do. A majority of the things that we do are done with the idea of winning approval of ourselves and of other people."

30

"Well, I believe that all of us need to have some person or persons who think a good deal of us. It gives us a sort of anchor in life to have people love us. Then, too, it keeps us unselfish if we think of others instead of ourselves," said Mrs. Chapman.

"You are certainly right, Mrs. Chapman," Mr. Newman said. "Take this matter of approval that all of us are so much concerned about. It is one of those things that are good for us if we have just enough, but bad if we have too much. We do not want to be so bound down by the desire to have others think well of us that we would not take a stand for the right in the face of criticism. The desire for praise is a fine thing when it makes us careful about being neat and clean and being polite to strangers as well as to our friends. This desire has some part even in our being honest and truthful. But we do not want it to be carried so far that we do not have any opinions of our own or simply follow the crowd because we are afraid of what they might say about us. Young people who are very susceptible often get into the habit of doing and saying what their group does and says, but sometimes they will stand up under criticism of both adults and people of their own age in order to do what they think is right. We hope to lead our boys and girls to desire above everything else the feeling that they have done what God approves of, rather than to be concerned chiefly with what

31

others say about them. This need of getting to higher and higher ideals begins with the baby who wants the approval of his mother and father. Later on he has playmates and children at school to think of, and gradually his circle of friends becomes larger. In each stage he must learn to rely more and more on what he thinks is the right thing to do rather than to follow the crowd. When we are working with boys and girls we must remember that this desire for approval, for the praise and admiration of others, is one of the most powerful things in life."

"I understand my boys better now, I think," Miss Hopkins said. "They were really trying to attract attention and show off when they were shooting paper wads last Sunday morning instead of wanting to bother me, as I imagined. They seemed to be trying to see who could shoot one the farthest, until I was tempted to dismiss them before the closing bell rang."

"Yes, each one was taking that way of trying to outdo the other fellow," Mr. Newman said. "Each wanted to feel that he could do better than the rest of the boys and to show the others what he could do. Sometimes a boy who cannot do well in school will try to shine by being very troublesome. He cannot win attention in any other way, so he uses the only thing that he can do easily—he gets the attention of both the teacher and the other pupils by being the 'worst boy' in the class or school. Of course he does not stop to think *why* he is acting this way. In fact, most boys and girls would not know why they act as they do, even if they did stop to think. Knowing that these wants are what make us behave as we do certainly helps us to understand ourselves and other people. These longings and desires lead us to do things without our reasoning about them. It would really take an effort on our part to keep from doing them. The fact that we are being 'carried along' by our desires is why they are called *drives* or *urges*. They are something within us that we are often not conscious of, but that accounts for our behavior. My knowledge of these things has been invaluable to me as a superintendent of day school and also of Sunday school, for it has made me able to help both pupils and teachers. When you can look beyond the thing a person does and see what makes him do it, you know better how to help that person."

"Let us think about those boys again," Miss Bonner suggested. "Was the desire to 'show off' the only reason why they cut up so much in class the other morning? It seems to me that often they get into trouble just because they are so full of energy and life that they simply can't keep still."

"I am glad you brought up that point, Miss Bonner," Mr. Newman said. "Frequently there are two or three

33

different wants or desires that make us do a certain thing. There were probably a number of reasons why the boys acted as they did, and we should try to find out as many of them as possible if we want to be sure that we understand the boys well. The whole class had to have some way of taking care of their longing to be active, as you have pointed out. Also they wanted to make things happen and to stir up some excitement. These wants, added to the desire to show off before each other, may have been the chief reasons why they behaved so badly, but perhaps there were others too."

Mr. Brown broke in here: "I agree with you about the boys wanting some excitement. Most of the young people to-day are spoiled, in my opinion. When I was a boy I was thrilled over my father's purchase of a second-hand surrey, and now a young fellow is not satisfied unless the family has an automobile which he can use himself most of the time. I lived five miles in the country, and I thought it was quite an event to go to town on Saturday, but boys that far from town these days think nothing of running in for a soda or a movie practically every day."

"Yes, ideas are certainly changing, but times have changed too," agreed Mr. Newman. "I venture that if we were about eighteen years old now we should feel just as the young people of to-day feel, but it is hard for us to realize that. These boys and girls have not had anything to say about the world in which they find themselves. This world has been made what it is chiefly because of what adults have done. I always have a sense of responsibility when I see young folks to-day facing a world that is different in so many ways from the one we faced thirty years ago when we were their age. I wonder how we would get along if we were young and had the problems they have to-day."

"I think that autos have done a great deal toward making people like change," Mrs. Sanders suggested. "Since it is so much easier to get around now than it was when we had only horses and buggies, most people take at least a few short trips, and many of them go off on long tours that were unheard of in my youth. We older people seem to like it pretty well ourselves, too. Even Mr. Brown here traveled in his car across two States to see his first grandson."

"Yes," Mr. Newman said, "all of us dread monotony, more or less, and want some adventure and change. Our neighbors are taking trips, and we become accustomed to do as they do. Furthermore, such trips satisfy our desire to *do* things. We feel that we have accomplished something when we have driven three hundred miles or more in one day, and we tell our friends proudly about how quickly we made the trip, and how far we went without a puncture, and how many miles we made on a gallon of gas. Also we like to make things happen, to be the cause of things, whether it be taking trips, or shooting paper wads, or tying a can on the tail of a stray dog, or raising a crop, or running a store, or building a house. We adults have a chance to do many things that we want to do, but the little boy who drives nails in the porch or draws pictures on the parlor wall is showing that he has the same desire to do things that we have, but does not use it to suit the older members of the family."

"Well, I suppose that liking to make things happen is really why I am pleased when I make a new kind of cake," said Mrs. Gordon. "I am never satisfied until I have a chance to try my hand at every new recipe that I can get hold of, for I do like to know that I can cook anything I want to. I feel the same way about making a dress or raising beautiful dahlias; I want to know that I *can* do it."

"The youth with his auto, the woman with her baking or her dressmaking, the man with his farming, the little boy with his popgun—all want to do something and to do it well," Mr. Newman said. "Children show this same desire when they want to put on their own coats or button their shoes, and even when they want to cross the road by themselves. In our Sunday school work we ought to use this desire to do things. Let the boys put the chairs in a row or put the songbooks on the benches at church time.

36

Even telling the story of the lesson is one way in which little children can 'do' something. The young people can put flowers in the church or act as ushers and be the officers in their own classes. This gives them something to do and also makes them feel important, so we are satisfying two wants in this way."

"Yes, and what they do for the Sunday school or the Church is training them to be thoughtful of others, is it not?" asked Mr. Brown.

"That is a good point," said Miss Bonner. "Most of us are interested in other folks, and I think we should use that interest. That explains why a number of us chose pictures of children or young people. One reason I enjoy my car so much is that I have a chance to give my friends pleasure by taking them out for rides. And I notice Mr. Gordon wanted a big car so that he could take all the family in it."

"As we said before, all of us are interested in other people, especially in those whom we love," said Mr. Newman. "One way of showing our love for them is to do things for them, just as Miss Bonner suggests. Another longing that we all have is for a feeling of security. You want to get to the place where you will not fear old age or dependence on other people. That is why there are so many advertisements in the magazines and papers about pensions and trust companies and endowment policies.

37

Not only do we want to feel secure and safe ourselves, but we are eager to provide for those whom we love in order that we may feel that they are safe too. We not only like to look forward to comfort in our old age, but we also want comfort and ease right now. Children and young people usually think only about the present; they are interested chiefly in what is happening to them to-day, and either do not think of to-morrow or do not bother about it. We learn to provide for the future. This feeling of living in the present is what makes it so hard for boys and girls to be interested when we say, 'Lay up for yourselves treasures in heaven.' They want something to-day, not something after they die."

"Sometimes when we are not satisfied with what we actually have to-day we may take it out in reading," Mr. Chester remarked. "I have not had a chance to travel much, and, like Miss Lane, I am always wanting to go on a long trip. I like to read stories in magazines and books about people who go around the world and see new sights and visit strange places. I can imagine that I am with them and feel almost as though I had taken a trip myself."

"That trick of imagining that one is the hero of the story is often indulged in by young people," said Mr. Newman. "They like romances and love stories because they have a chance to imagine that they are just like the beauti-

38

ful women or handsome men in the tales they are reading. When they are not reading stories they are often daydreaming, thinking of themselves as being very popular or very charming or very smart or very good or very great in some way. They get a lot of satisfaction from this, and it is hard for them when they are called back to earth and have to wash the dishes or hoe the potatoes. If we were honest about our own daydreams, we would probably find out that each of us here sometimes imagines how it would feel to be a great person in some way. Now, this dreaming is a very good thing when it leads us to do something. It shows that we have imagination. I believe that inventors and explorers and authors, like Edison and Byrd and Shakespeare, must have imagined things and had their dreams before they did things. But it is a bad thing to dream too much, trying to build up an imaginary world where everything is just as one wants it. In real life often things are *not* just as we would like to have them be. We must learn to accept some things as they are and make the best of them. We must face facts and find out some way either to change things or to make the best of them. Instead of doing this, we often try to forget or ignore the facts, or we attempt to make up an excuse for sliding out of some of our difficulties."

"We have been talking about so many interests and

39

longings and wants that I have become somewhat lost," Miss Lane protested. "I want to think all these things through more carefully later on, and I believe it would help me if we should prepare a list of them."

"That is a good idea," Mr. Newman responded. "I will write on the board if all of you will call out the things that you have learned that all of us want. Now let us make a list."

The members of the group named the following wants or desires:

> To accomplish something; to do things; to make things happen.
> To feel important; to attract attention; to win the admiration of others.
> Interest in others—family, friends, children, old people.
> Love; interest in the other sex.
> Possession; owning things.
> Comfort, ease, security.
> Travel and adventure; excitement.
> Activity; play and games.
> Curiosity; wonder.
> Sympathy (caused by interest in others).
> Satisfaction of hunger and bodily needs.

"That is a pretty good list, isn't it?" Mr. Newman said. "Now, instead of answering the questions that Miss Hopkins raised again at the beginning of our discussion to-night, I wish that you would think over carefully all the things that we have been talking about and see if you can

40

notice in your pupils next Sunday any signs of these long-ings and desires. If we understand better just why our pupils act as they do, perhaps we shall be able to work with them better. And remember that often a person does a thing not for one reason alone, but for two or three reasons. As we said before, there are sometimes a number of wishes or longings or desires that lead a person to behave as he does. Next week we can talk over all these things again."

CHAPTER III

WHAT ARE THEY INTERESTED IN?
(CONTINUED)

"It is fine that all of our officers and teachers are here again this week," Mr. Brown said. "From what some of them have been telling me, Mr. Newman, I am sure that they will have a number of questions to ask, as well as a number of interesting reports to make."

"Since you were the one to raise the first problem last week, Miss Hopkins, suppose you tell us what happened in your class last Sunday," Mr. Newman said.

"I did not realize how little I knew about my boys until I began watching them as you suggested last week," Miss Hopkins confessed. "I was at the building about twenty minutes before Sunday school opened, and the first boy who came in was James. He has always been hard to manage, and he is the leader in playing pranks in class. I saw that he had something in one of his pockets, and I asked him what it was. His face lighted up, and he pulled out a sack of marbles and showed them to me. Some of them were very pretty, and I picked up one and said: 'This is a beautiful taw; I should like to try to shoot it.' He looked very much surprised and asked me if I had ever played with marbles. 'O, yes,' I replied, 'my brother, who was only a year older than I, taught me how to play, but I have forgotten a good deal about it. I should like to watch you play sometime, however.' 'Well,' he said with a grin, 'I did not know that you could do anything like that. Come see me play some day. I can beat anybody in our crowd.' I told him I was glad to hear it, and promised to see him this week. Then I suggested that his marbles were very pretty, and if the other boys saw them they would be so interested that they would not settle down to the lesson, and I asked him what he thought we should do. 'I'll not let the fellows see mine until after class, and they had better not try to show any of theirs while you are teaching us, either. You just leave it to me.' The lesson went off beautifully. James would frown at any boy who began whispering or who was not paying attention to what the others were saying. One boy rolled a paper wad and shot it across the room before James knew what he was doing. 'Hey, cut that out!' he commanded. The boy was so astonished that he did not answer. After class I thanked James privately for helping me, and he said: 'O, that's all right.' And off he ran to join the others."

"Did you think through the reasons why James acted as he did, Miss Hopkins?" Mr. Newman inquired.

"I have spent all my spare time trying to figure that

43

out, and I was surprised to find how many interests and wants he showed even in that one incident. He owned the marbles and was pleased to possess them. They were his very own. He could 'do things' with them, which means that they appealed to his desire to be active and to 'make things happen.' Even though he did not show them to the other boys, he brought them with that idea, for he hoped to make the others admire him, or even envy him, because he had so many of them and such pretty ones. He was glad to have me show that I liked his possessions, and he swelled with pride as he told me that he could 'beat all the other fellows.' This same desire for praise and recognition was shown when he boasted that he could make the boys in the class behave. He felt important when *he* kept order in the class. He got the attention of the class by 'keeping them straight,' just as he had gotten it before this by being the leader in playing pranks."

"You have figured out his interests very well, Miss Hopkins," Mr. Newman said. "Do any of the others in our group want to ask any questions?"

"I have been wondering if James was not actually 'doing something' when he kept the other boys quiet," Miss Bonner suggested. "We usually think of being active only when we are walking or plowing or weaving or doing something with our bodies, but I have decided that we are really active when we are thinking, also. When I was at college I used to feel as though I had done a day's work after I had studied hard; it wore me out. So we are really leading our pupils to be active when we lead them to think and to give their attention to the discussion. That is what I feel about the young people in my class: they are taking part in the work when they talk about their problems and how they should be met. Am I right in this?"

"Yes, it is not only physical activity that we are interested in," Mr. Newman said. "The members of the adult class do not leave their seats and pass story papers and paste pictures in books and draw on the board as the little folks do, but they are having a part in the class if they join in the discussion, or even listen to others. Children who stay in the house and read on a rainy day are mentally active, too, though if they are quiet too long it probably means that they are not well. That is a good point, Miss Bonner."

"I believe that just because James was interested in keeping the other boys quiet last Sunday it is not certain that he will always try to keep them quiet," Mrs. Gordon remarked. "He felt that he was a partner of the teacher that one day, and he found pleasure in doing this because it was something new. Also he liked to show Miss Hopkins that he could 'boss' the boys, but I suspect that she will have the same old trouble with him sooner or later."

"That is certainly true," Miss Hopkins said. "I am not

45

hoping that James will be a model boy from now on, but I found out one of his interests. He realizes that I can be his friend and that I am 'human,' as he would probably put it. I am encouraged because our discussion last week helped me to understand him better. I see now that I should be a companion to the boys—study the boys themselves rather than merely study the Sunday school lesson and ask questions on it. The fact that I could keep James interested for even one Sunday makes me feel that I could interest him on other Sundays if I knew him better. So I am glad to come to these meetings of our Sunday School Council, and I warn you that I will ask a lot of questions each week."

"You spoke of James not being a 'model boy,'" Mrs. Chapman said. "I have noticed that grown people usually think a child is a good child when he does not bother them. We are too liable to think about ourselves and our comfort instead of thinking about the children and how they are developing. Rearing children is no easy or comfortable job, and in order to do it well one has to give time and thought and effort to it. I think that the same thing is true of teaching a Sunday school class. We must be willing to find out the needs of our pupils and then do what we can to meet those needs, instead of deciding what we think the children should know and then trying to make them learn it."

"I agree with you," said Mr. Chester, "but it is some-times very hard to know just what those needs are, as I said at our first meeting. For instance, in my class of young people there was very little interest in the lesson last Sunday. One of the girls had given a party the eve-ning before, and the others had gone to it. They were so busy whispering to each other and passing notes and teas-ing Bill and Margaret, who have quite a 'case,' that they would pay no attention to me. They are just downright rude and thoughtless, and I don't know what to do. I realize that each one is interested in the other sex, but why do they carry on like that?"

"Perhaps they have not had an opportunity to see each other much and are in need of more parties or good times together," Mr. Newman suggested. "Then, too, there is a certain amount of excitement or thrill in doing some-thing that is more or less forbidden, and they enjoy the feeling that they are running things. If they were made responsible themselves for the order in the class, if they could feel that it is *their* class and that they are managing it themselves, some of the trouble might disappear. It would take a rather long time to teach them how to organ-ize and carry on the class work, but it would be very worth while in the end. Let them be the officers, with you as the adult adviser. Of course they may do things somewhat poorly at first, but they will never know how to be re-

47

sponsible until they have some experiences in carrying responsibilities. Do you see any other reasons for these suggestions of mine?"

"Yes," Mr. Chester replied. "I suppose that such a plan would make them feel that they were important, that they were accomplishing things themselves, and then each one would do his best so that he would win the approval of the group."

"I think the desire to win the approval of others is one of the strongest urges or longings that we have," Miss Lane put in. "In my class of Juniors I have discovered that frequently a boy or girl will be more influenced by the opinion of the other members of the class than by my opinion. Now that I understand better just how they feel, I shall try to guide the children in their thinking and in forming their own opinions. I remember now something I read some weeks ago but paid little attention to at the time. In a certain magazine article the author recommended that the children in a class decide on their own rules, because then they would make each other stand by these rules much more than if the teacher herself had merely told them what to do. Is this a plan which can be worked in Sunday school?"

"I am sure it can, for I have tried it out to some extent," Mrs. Chapman said. "There were two children in my class who always came to Sunday school early so that they could put their chairs next to mine. Finally the others began fussing about it. 'I want one of those seats sometimes,' Jane wailed. 'I come with my sister, and she won't leave soon enough for me to get here before Catherine and Isabel come, and it is not fair for them to have those seats *every* Sunday.' So we all talked it over together, and the children themselves decided that they should take turn about. It has proved to be a very good plan."

"I have always carried out that idea in my home with my own children," Mrs. Gordon said. "They have a real sense of honor and fairness; and if one takes advantage of the others, they all jump on him and make him fall into line. I always thought it was better to have an agreement like that than for parents to make a lot of rules themselves and then force children to follow them. I believe the reason this plan works so well is that it gives children a chance to 'do things' themselves; they feel important because they have accomplished something."

"And the group spirit is very useful in carrying out the plan," Mr. Brown said. "In reading about the Boy Scouts I learned that out of every hundred boys between the ages of eleven and fourteen, about eighty-five are in clubs or gangs or some sort of organization. And the boys are greatly influenced by the others in the group. If the gang is made up of the right kind of boys, it is fine for them. But sometimes a good boy may join a gang of boys who are rough and who may even lie and cheat and steal, and then it is a dangerous thing. We must take account of the fact that boys want to be with each other in this way, and I think it is an excellent plan to organize all the Sunday school classes above the juniors and let the boys and girls be the officers and carry on the work just as Mr. Newman suggested for Mr. Chester's young people."

"Yes, and I think the girls should do the same thing," said Mrs. Chapman. "They are very much like the boys in most ways, and they should be taught to take over certain responsibilities. But I should like to know why they are all so eager to have clubs or gangs. What wants and desires are at the root of that feeling?"

"After all, even adults like to be with each other," Mr. Newman remarked. "In cities and towns there is nearly always a Lions' Club or a Rotary Club or some other organization of business and professional men. And if the women were frank, they would probably confess that they enjoy the missionary society meetings not only because they have a chance to work for missions, but also because they like to see and talk with each other about their new clothes and new recipes and a neighbor's sickness, and how well their children are doing in school, and what bargains they have bought, and how their gardens are growing, and how many chickens they have hatched off, and the price of eggs. And through all of their conversation you will find that each one is proud of *her* recipe and *her* children and the bargains *she* found, and so on. I see you men are smiling, but you act just the same way: if you are a farmer and are not able to boast about a specially good crop, you get attention and sympathy by complaining about what the drought did to your prospects for a good crop of corn. Or if you are a weaver you talk about how many yards of cloth you ran off or how some of the spindles or looms are out of fix, which accounts for the shortage in this week's record. So the desire to attract the attention of others and to think well of oneself is strong within each one of us and shows itself in most of the things that we say and do. We adults try to win the approval of our group just as the boys and girls do, though we may not have a club or any organized group."

"This discussion has interested me, but I want some help about my own class," Miss Lane said. "On Sunday, Margaret, a timid, quiet little girl in my class, brought her doll whose clothes she had made. She knows how to sew beautifully, but of course it was rather disturbing to have all the children playing with the doll rather than paying attention as they should. I let them look at the doll long

51

enough to satisfy their curiosity, and then persuaded them to let Dolly go to sleep while we went on with our work. But why do you think the child brought it to the class? She has always been so shy and retiring that I was surprised at this."

"That very shyness and quietness is probably what made her bring the doll," Mr. Newman explained. "In the first place, she showed her longing to make something, to create, by making the dress; she took delight in that activity. Then, since she is so bashful that she does not have much attention, she took this way of gaining it. She was undoubtedly very popular there for a while, when each little girl was begging for a chance to hold the doll. She enjoyed the fact that the group admired something she possessed and also admired her ability to sew. Of course she was not conscious of all this, but if you will watch little children closely you will often find them doing things to attract attention, just as grown-ups do."

"There is one question I want to ask," Mrs. Ray said. "You have said that we like to be active and that we want to attract the attention of others. If that is so, how do you account for the fact that in a class of adults the members refuse to take part in the discussion and will not have a teacher who does not lecture without asking them questions?"

"One reason why most adults will not join in the class discussion is that they are in the habit of listening to the teacher, and they do not want to exert themselves," Mr. Newman explained. "They prefer to be 'entertained' instead of doing some real thinking themselves. Then, too, they are often a bit nervous about talking, because they feel that they may make a statement that will not win the approval of the group. Sometimes there are certain men or women who make themselves nuisances by talking a great deal. They are getting attention in this way, and some of them seem to enjoy attention even at the price of making themselves more or less unpopular. However, there are many folks who enjoy lectures in Sunday school rather than taking part in a class discussion. As I have just pointed out, most of us do not want to attract attention unless it is favorable. That is one reason why we do not want to attempt things we have never done before and are not sure we can do well. We want to 'shine' in everything that we undertake. Watch for this feeling on the part of the people whom you are with, and you will be surprised to see how often you find it."

"I believe there is another desire or interest which has something to do with this," Miss Bonner suggested. "When we undertake something new we have a feeling of insecurity, and we said last week that we all want comfort and a sense of being secure. The feeling of not being sure

53

of oneself might keep us from doing things ranging from changing from one business to another down to trying to play games at a party. It is interesting to see how more than one desire or urge is found as the cause of most things that we do."

"I am glad you brought up that point, Miss Bonner," Mr. Newman said. "I wish that we had more time to talk about other interests and longings that were shown by our pupils last Sunday. Of course there are many other points that we should take up, but some of these we will talk about later on. We cannot take up each of these interests and wants in turn and see in detail how it should be used in Sunday school work. However, since we have discussed the longings and desires that people have and how all these wants make people act as they do, I hope that we shall be able to see beyond the behavior of our pupils to the *reasons for* their behaving as they do. Only when we are able to do this will we be able to guide our pupils well. When we try to make people do things that run against these desires and longings we get into trouble. These wants are part of the nature that a person is born with. Therefore we are working with God when we take these wants into account, while we may be working against him when we disregard them."

"Do you mean that all of human nature is good and that we do not have to try to change people in any way, but simply let them follow their own wishes or desires?" Mr. Morris asked.

"No, indeed," Mr. Newman hastened to say. "Practically all these longings and desires can be used either for good or for evil. For example, the wish to possess things may show itself in wanting to earn money so that one can help one's aged parents or other people, or it may lead a person to despise his fellow man and become a miser. Again, we want men who have firm convictions and who will not be turned aside by any difficulties that they run up against. A child will not become a man of this sort if his parents try to 'break his will' and do not give him an opportunity to carry out his own ideas to some extent. On the other hand, a child with a strong desire to have his own way may be given in to until he becomes a tyrant, and when he is a man he cannot have the right attitude toward his wife and children and will not be able to carry on his business successfully. Some of our longings must be held in check or must be turned into new directions. For example, the woman who has no children may be led through her 'mother love' to become the matron of an orphans' home and look after the children of others. It is the hope of religious education that we may be able to guide these urges and longings in such a way that they will make for a full Christian character. This guidance must begin early in the child's life, for what happens to the little child will

55

have a lasting effect on him. I trust that our discussions in this group will lead us to see how we may become better able to guide our pupils in their growth in Christian character. In order to do this, we must know their different interests; so let us all continue to study our pupils carefully."

CHAPTER IV

HOW DO THEY LEARN?

"The thing that I need most help on is how to get the children in my class to learn the Sunday school lesson each week," said Miss Lane. "I have tried everything that I know. I have begged them to do it, and I have scolded them, and I have offered them prizes, but I don't seem to get anywhere with them."

"What lesson did you have last Sunday, Miss Lane?" asked Mr. Newman.

"It was on truthfulness, but my boys and girls could not answer half the questions."

"Well, suppose they could answer *all* the questions—"

"My, that surely would be fine!"

"Yes, it would mean that they could at least *recite* the lesson and that they had learned the answers to the questions in the book. When you were a child you used to say that you had 'learned' a poem or 'piece' that you were to 'say' before your class or school, but you were merely repeating what you had memorized. But why do you try to teach a lesson on truthfulness?"

"I want them to learn to tell the truth, of course."

"Do you have in your class a boy on whose word you cannot depend, one who has lied to you?"

"Yes, I have caught Will telling lies a number of times, and I wanted him to learn this lesson particularly."

"Did you ask Will any questions on the lesson?"

"Yes, I did that on purpose; and now that I come to think of it, he could answer more questions than any of the others."

"Do you believe this means that he had learned the lesson of truthfulness better than the others had?"

"Well, I don't know. I was pleased that he could answer the questions, and I'd say that he had learned what I was trying to teach him. But perhaps I was teaching just answers to questions."

"I believe we shall have to try to see if there is not more to learning than that," said Mr. Newman. "Let us see how you learn to do something yourself. Your father has just bought a car, and you want to drive it. You ask him to teach you how to drive it, and he tells you about the steering wheel and the gears and the clutch and all the other things that you need to know in order to be able to drive. Then to be sure that you understand what he has told you, he asks you questions. You are able to answer all of them—how to start and stop, how to use the clutch and the brake, and all the rest. Are you then ready to take out a license as a driver?"

"I should say not! Father did tell me about how to drive a car before ours was delivered. He was not at home when the agent brought it out to us. After the man left I tried to start it. I was sure that I was doing just the right thing, but it suddenly lurched backward and ran into a tree. Father told me later that I had put the gear into reverse instead of low. Then he showed me how to start, to shift gears, and to stop. I did these things under his direction until I got a pretty good idea of how to manage the car. I have been practicing for some days now, and I think that I will drive it alone to-morrow."

"When you got into the car with your father, did you notice the gear shift the first thing?"

"I surely did. I did not want to back into the tree again, so I was very careful about shifting. Under father's direction I shifted correctly and was pleased to have the car start forward. Then I shifted again and again, and I soon learned to do it pretty well."

"We see clearly that in learning to do something such as driving a car we have to *do the thing instead of merely talking about it*. The talking about how to drive was not enough. You had to get into the car and *do* all the things about which you had been talking. Also you repeated the things that were successful, and you were careful not to repeat the things that were unsuccessful. When you found that shifting the gear in a certain way meant that the car would go backward you tried out another way of

59

shifting, then you found one that was a success and were pleased with this success. Furthermore, you did not make just one trial and then decide that you were an expert driver. It will take a lot of practice on your part to be able to handle the car as easily as your father does, as you realize. Do you understand more clearly now how people learn things?"

"Yes," Miss Lane answered. "I had never tried to think it through before. I see that there are two chief points to be remembered: you have to do the thing again and again, and you will repeat only those things that make you glad that you did them."

"This discussion that you two have had has helped all of us, I am sure," Mrs. Gordon said. "But there is one thing that puzzles me. I learned to make a marble cake the other day, and I had no trouble at all in learning to do it. The first one I made was delicious, and I am confident that I could make another one just as good to-morrow. I did not have to try my hand at it again and again. Now, can you say that I learned to make that kind of cake in just *one* trial?"

"Have you ever made other kinds of cake?" Mr. Newman asked.

"Mrs. Gordon is noted for her cooking, Mr. Newman," Mr. Morris hastened to say. "You are a newcomer here, or you would not ask that question."

"I felt sure that you were a good hand at making cakes, Mrs. Gordon, because what you said shows that," Mr. Newman said. "You have had much experience with recipes and with mixing batter and with baking. There were not many things about the cake that were really new to you, because you were familiar with the principles of cake-making, and simply used some new ingredients. The amount of practice that you need will depend on how much you know about what you are trying to learn. Now, the situation would have been quite different if you had tried to learn something that was entirely strange to you, such as using a typewriter."

"You selected a good example," said Mrs. Gordon with a laugh. "I tried to use the typewriter Thomas bought recently and soon gave it up because I couldn't hit the right keys. I don't see how people can write so fast on the contrary machines."

"You feel that way because you have not practiced long enough. If you tried it again and again, you might learn to type easily and quickly," Mr. Newman reassured her.

"May we go back to a discussion of Will and my difficulty with him?" Miss Lane asked. "What you have said throws light on the problem. I see that I have been thinking that when my pupils could answer the questions I asked them about a lesson they had therefore learned the lesson. But Will, for example, has not *learned* the *lesson* on truthfulness until he tells the truth."

"Perhaps it will help us to understand the case better if we try to imagine why Will began telling lies," Mr. Newman suggested. "I have heard that Will's father and mother were very stern and used to punish him severely when he was just a little boy. Suppose his mother asked him one day who took the little cakes she had put on a plate in the pantry. Now, Will had eaten the cakes himself, but he was afraid of being punished, so he said the neighbor's boy who was playing with him that afternoon took them. His mother may have said: 'That child is a nuisance, and I do not want him over here playing with you.' Will heaved a sigh of relief and was delighted that he had so easily escaped punishment. The next week he may have lost his father's knife and have been questioned about that. On insisting that he knew nothing about it, he escaped punishment again and was again pleased over it. After lying like this again and again, he finally came to the point where he was ready to tell a lie instead of the truth whenever he found himself in a tight place. To him it was much more satisfying to tell a lie and not be punished than to tell the truth and be punished. The chief thing to be remembered about this is the fact that he learned to do whatever was most pleasing or satisfying to him, and that he learned it only after he had tried it

62

out again and again. We say now that he has a habit of telling lies; this habit was built up as he learned."

"I believe we are getting still further light on just what learning means," said Mrs. Sanders. "But there is one thing that I have been wondering about: you say that we do the thing that pleases or satisfies us. But I do not think it is very pleasant to take the blame about a thing when we have told the truth about it, even if we know that we are not to be punished for it. I will tell the truth when I find myself in a tight place, but it is not pleasant. I think your reasoning falls down there."

"How would you feel about yourself if you told a lie?"

"I am sure that I should not be able to sleep at night if I did that. It would be against all my ideals and principles," Mrs. Sanders protested.

Mr. Newman smiled. "Then have you not answered your own question? *Why* do you tell the truth even when it is embarrassing and when it may get you into trouble? It is because you have a set of ideals that are so strong that it would be less pleasing to you to do anything contrary to these ideals than to suffer from telling the truth. In other words, telling the truth and suffering for it is better, in your opinion, than telling a lie, even though you might thus escape blame or punishment. As in so many things, it is really a matter of choice. Will has not yet built up a set of ideals that make him feel unhappy when he tells a lie. He is interested in what is going to happen to him right away, and he is apt to choose the easiest way out of a situation because that is what will please him best. It is the task of his teachers, now that his parents are dead, to see that he gets more pleasure from telling the truth than from telling a lie. Habit is so strong with him that it will be difficult to get him to the point where he prefers to tell the truth. If telling the truth becomes more pleasing to him than telling lies, he will tell the truth, but not until then."

"But how can I help him do this?" Miss Lane asked.

"That will depend on what kind of boy Will is, on how the other boys feel toward him, on what his teachers in day school do for him, and on other things also. Each boy must be treated differently because he is different from all others, and you must know him well so that you may understand what help he needs. But I do know that you will never be able to do anything with him, or with any other boy who is a liar, until telling the truth brings more pleasure than telling lies brings. You can do something for him in your Sunday school class, but you should be with him during the week also. Whenever he does tell the truth, be sure to praise him for it and make him pleased that he did not lie. The best way to break him of the habit of lying is to help him form the habit of telling the truth. The more often he tells the truth, the better; for the oftener we do a thing, the more apt we are to continue doing it—provided, of course, that the doing satisfies us. Practice is absolutely necessary, and it is just as important to have pleasure come from the practice as it is to have practice. Perhaps a good slogan for us would be, 'Practice with Satisfaction,' as one teacher put it."

"I see where I have been making a mistake with my little girl who is so careless about putting away her clothes," said Mrs. Ray. "I have been scolding her whenever she forgot to do it, but I have not often praised her when she remembered to do it. After all, praise is cheap, and yet we rarely use it. I am going to see what praising her will do."

"I think you are very wise, Mrs. Ray," remarked Mr. Newman. "However, give the plan a good long trial before you become discouraged. Often we give up too soon because we do not see good results so soon as we think we should. It takes a world of patience to help children learn things either in the home or in Sunday school. How many of you have ever said, 'It is easier for me to do that myself than to try to teach you to do it'?"

A number of the group smiled. "I am sure all of us have been guilty of that," confessed Miss Hopkins. "Two years ago when my little sister wanted to learn to make a dress, and I promised to teach her, I could hardly keep myself from taking the material away from her and working on it myself. However, I tried to be patient and let her do the cutting and sewing herself while I showed her how to do it. The dress was quite a success, and she was so pleased with it that she wanted to keep on sewing, so she made an apron for me as a surprise. She was doing just what you suggested to us. She 'practiced with satisfaction.' And now she can sew as well as I can, though it did take her a long time to learn."

"Another very important thing for us to remember when we are trying to teach a person to do something is that he must have some real reason for learning to do it. Why do you like to sew, Miss Hopkins?" asked Mr. Newman.

"First, because I want some pretty clothes, and it is cheaper to make them than it is to buy them. Then I like to accomplish something, as we said in our discussion some weeks ago. I am pleased when I have done a thing well."

"I like to cook because I can do it well," said Mrs. Gordon, "and because I want to have good food for my family."

"I try to run my farm well in order to make a good

living for my family, and also because I take pride in being a successful farmer," said Mr. Gordon.

"In every case we will find that there is some want or desire or interest that leads us to do a thing," Mr. Newman pointed out. "Sometimes an interest is so strong with a woman that we say she has her 'mind set' on a certain thing. Her mind may be set on a new dress or on a car or on spring cleaning or on sending her daughter to school. Whatever it is, she will do everything she can to get what she wants. Sometimes a man will set his mind on doing a certain thing, such as learning a new business, and he will work at it until he learns it. A boy may be 'ready' to learn to throw a ball well, because he is pitcher for his team. A girl is ready and eager to learn to drive a car so that she can take trips to town without depending on some one else to do the driving. Her father would say, 'The child has her heart set on doing it.' Now, having a mind set to do a thing is very important. Unless there is something within us that is urging us to do it, may not be done. We forget this, however, when we want children to learn things. 'Why?' is a question that they ask us more often than we like. There is always a *why,* or reason, for the things that *we* do, but we expect children to do things just because we tell them to do so without stopping to think about whether they are interested or ready. In some cases we are right in making them do certain things, but often if we helped them to the place where they would *want* to do other things, it would be much easier on them and on us. Besides, they would learn much more readily."

"How does that apply to the case of Will and our trying to get him to tell the truth?" asked Miss Lane.

"There is certainly a reason why Will has been lying when he gets into a tight place," Mr. Newman answered. "He has found that usually he is not blamed or punished when he lies. Sometimes he has been caught and punished for lying, but that merely makes him sorry that he was caught, not sorry that he lied. But since he is usually pleased by the results of his lying, that gives him a good reason to keep on doing it. Now, he is not going to change from lying to telling the truth unless there is some reason for it, unless he is 'ready on the inside'—not being made to do it, but preferring to do it. Until he has a 'readiness' to do it, he will not do it. If he is afraid only of being punished, his mind is set, not on telling the truth, but on escaping the punishment, and he will tell the truth only when he fears that he will be caught if he lies. We want him to be ready to tell the truth at all times, no matter what will happen when he does it."

"Would stories about heroes help him decide to tell the truth?" Miss Lane queried.

"They would surely help some if Will felt that he was

68

likely to be in a place such as the hero was in. Will may be able to tell the story of Washington and the cherry tree, and yet it might not have any effect upon him. However, if he knows that the best business men in town, the bankers and the farmers and the ones who own the stores, are successful because other people trust them and can depend on their word, he may realize that it is a wise plan to tell the truth because it helps a boy or man 'get on' in life. But we want Will to be truthful, not merely because it is wise, but because it is right. He must be helped to build up high ideals. And if one of these men could be his hero, and Will wanted to be like him, this would help change Will. He would then have a mind set on being like his hero and would have a good start toward telling the truth. This is one thing that we try to do in our classes in Sunday school—to inspire pupils to tell the truth. One of the best ways to do this is to lead the boy to realize that you think well of him, that you believe in him and depend on him. To appeal to his pride, to try to get him to live up to the highest that is in him, to help him feel that he *can* be what God wants him to be, and that God himself is Truth—all of these things are needed. We have found out, however, that this is only the first step. After he feels all this, he must go farther. Merely wanting to do it or talking about it is not enough; he must actually *do* it."

"In thinking over what we have been talking about, it seems to me that there are three things that we must remember," said Miss Bonner.

"First, we must help our pupils come to the point where they are ready to learn without being forced to do it, where they have their minds set to learn.

"Second, we have to see to it that the pupils practice what they are to learn.

"Third, we must see that they are satisfied with what they are trying to do, that they have a feeling of success and not failure.

"If any one of these things is left out, our children cannot learn as they should. As I recollect, that is the way habits are built, is it not?"

"You are right, Miss Bonner," Mr. Newman agreed. "A habit is really the result of having learned a thing so well that you do that thing without stopping to think about it. I believe we scarcely realize how much of our life is habit. One well-known teacher of psychology said that nine hundred and ninety-nine out of every thousand things that we do are really habits. Not only our walking and talking and plowing and weaving and cooking, but even our thinking is usually merely habit."

"Isn't it a good thing that this is true?" Mr. Morris asked. "I have been helping my little boy as he learns to dress himself, and I have often thought how little I could accomplish if I had to give as much attention as he does to a thing as simple as putting on one's clothes. He has to struggle with the buttons and with his shoes, and his fingers seem to be all thumbs."

"It certainly saves time for us to be able to form so many habits," Mr. Newman said, "but we must remember that after we form them we become more or less slaves to them. For that reason it is very important that only the right habits are formed. People often speak of bad habits and forget to mention the good ones that a person has. We say that a boy has a habit of slamming doors or a girl has a habit of not hanging up her clothes, but we forget that not making too much of bumps and cuts, and being polite to strangers, and building up high ideals can also be made into habits. In fact, if we do anything often enough it is likely to become a habit—provided, of course, that satisfaction comes from having done it, as we have pointed out so often to-night. We could give many evenings to a discussion of this one topic; but since we cannot give that much time to it, we will refer to habits often when we are talking about other topics. And whenever you want to ask a question about forming habits please feel free to do so."

CHAPTER V

THEY LEARN MORE THAN ONE THING AT A TIME

"Do you think that a person could learn more than one thing at a time, Miss Lane?" asked Mr. Newman.

"I don't believe he could," Miss Lane replied. "If he began thinking about other things, it seems to me that it would keep him from learning the very thing he set out to learn."

"Does one ever learn things without thinking about them?"

"I don't know that, either. Let me see how it would work in my class. I am trying to get my children to memorize the Twenty-Third Psalm, and I don't believe they can do that without really thinking about it."

"It may be rather easy to lead them to memorize the Psalm so that they can recite it without making any errors, but while they are trying to remember the words are they learning anything else?"

"I do not know what they would learn along with the words of the Psalm," said Mrs. Gordon, "but I do know that while Tom was working on his problems in arithmetic this winter he learned to dislike his teacher. He got along fine with his teacher last year and led his class in 'math,' but he says that the new teacher is not fair, and he is at the point where he hates even arithmetic, though it used to be his favorite subject."

"That is a good illustration," said Mr. Newman. "We are learning, or building up, ways of acting and feeling toward people and subjects while we are learning other things. And these ways of feeling and acting—or attitudes, as we might call them—are more important than knowing any number of problems in arithmetic, or poems, or history dates, or the exports of America. Tom probably likes school less now than he did before. While he was working the problems, he was learning to dislike arithmetic and his teacher and school and studying, and it is more serious that he has formed a distaste for these things than it would be if he did not know his 'math' lesson. We never learn just one thing at a time, and these 'extra' learnings that I have been talking about, these side learnings that go along with the learning that the teacher and the child are thinking of, are often the chief things."

"All that never did occur to me before," Mrs. Sanders said. "It makes teaching harder than ever when you think about that. Just seeing that children are in their places at Sunday school is certainly not enough. I have always been interested chiefly in having them recite their memory verses and bring a penny or so for the offering, but this opens up a really new idea to me."

73

"We teachers have to be particularly careful about what our pupils learn concerning the Sunday school and the Church," Mr. Newman responded. "If a child comes to Sunday school and finds that the place is not clean, that the building needs to be painted, that the songbooks are soiled and torn, and that the teacher does not prepare her lesson, what is he learning about Sunday school? He will believe that the members of the Church do not think that religion and the Church are so important as their own homes or their cars or farms. There will grow up in him, without his knowing it, a lack of respect for the Church and for religion itself. The way Miss Lane acts toward Will while she is trying to teach him to tell the truth or to memorize the Twenty-Third Psalm will have a great deal to do with what he learns about truthfulness and about the Bible. Suppose that while she was talking about truthfulness she scolded him before the other members of the class and called him a liar (though, of course, we know that she would never do this). The discomfort that he would feel would not be attached to his lying, but would probably lead him to think of the Sunday school as a place where he was made uncomfortable and of teachers as very unpleasant persons. He might come to dislike Sunday school and all that it stands for. But when Miss Lane shows her trust in him and praises him when he

74

tells the truth, he will feel that it is a pleasure to come to Sunday school and to be in her class."

"I've been thinking about what my children will learn while they memorize the Twenty-Third Psalm," said Miss Lane. "If I offered a prize and only one child won it, the others might be filled with resentment and learn to hate the winner. Perhaps they would even begin to dislike the Psalms or the Bible itself. I had not realized that there were so many things to consider."

"One of the strange things about attitudes, or how you feel and act toward things, is that you can carry them over from certain things to other things," said Miss Bonner. "For example, when Thomas learned to dislike his teacher he learned also to dislike arithmetic because he thought of the two together. Often you cannot remember what makes you hate a thing, and could not give a reason for feeling as you do. Perhaps you have a favorite color or flower that you think of in connection with a certain person. As for me, I am sure that my love for daffodils was brought about by the fact that I used to pick them early in the spring at our old home. And now my favorite color is yellow."

"Some very interesting experiments have been carried on in finding how people form likes and dislikes of both things and persons," Mr. Newman said. "Babies are frightened by loud noises and often cry and show other signs of fear when they hear them. Peter, a little boy who had a pet rabbit, was given the rabbit one day just as some one near by struck a steel bar with a piece of iron. Peter was startled, but began playing with his pet. On the next day the bar was struck again just as the rabbit was handed to him. He drew back and began to whimper, but took the rabbit later on. On the next day, when the same thing happened, Peter refused to take the rabbit, and ran away from it instead. Finally the very sight of the rabbit that he had loved so much before was enough to make Peter cry and run away, even though the loud noise was not made. Now, the fear of the loud sound was carried over from the noise to the rabbit because the two had come together so often that the sight of one made him act just as he did when he saw the other. Perhaps you have had something like this happen to you. Do you love certain places because you had a good time there?"

"Yes," Mrs. Ray said. "Some distance from my old home there was a tiny lake with an island in it. My grandfather used to take us children over there to let us play, and we had wonderful times wading and catching crawfishes and pretending that we were shipwrecked on the island. I love the place yet because of having enjoyed it so much then."

"I had an experience in school when I was in the fourth

grade that made me positively hate the little country school that I was attending at that time," Mr. Morris said. "I memorized a poem to speak at the close of school. I have forgotten the poem, but I remember only too well that it was rather sentimental and that a group of big boys at the back of the room laughed at me when I recited it. I went to another school in the fall, which was a good thing, because I do not believe that I could ever again have done well at the first school. I used to go half a mile out of my way to avoid passing that schoolhouse, because my pride had been so hurt by those boys that even seeing the building made a lump rise up in my throat."

"I shall always like Longfellow's poems because I loved the English teacher who taught them to me, but one of my chums did not like the teacher and disliked not only Longfellow but all other poets for some years," Mr. Newman added. "All this shows how attitudes are formed and how we learn a number of things at one time. If a baby is hurt in any way by a doctor, the very sight of the doctor is enough to make the baby cry. He was hurt and cried when the doctor vaccinated him, and now simply a glimpse of the doctor makes the baby yell. A boy who is not studious may be forced to study and be turned against books and the schoolhouse and the teachers or other people who try to make him study. On the other hand, a child who has a teacher whom he loves very much will transfer or carry over part of that love to the school and his experiences in it. That is one reason why it is very important to have fine, attractive teachers for our Sunday school classes. A child who dislikes her Sunday school teacher, or who is made to feel uncomfortable in church, may finally hate church and Sunday school."

"That really links up with what we had to say about learning, does it not?" asked Mrs. Gordon. "If you forced a child to go to church every Sunday, he would not have a *habit* of going because he was not pleased with the way going to church made him feel."

"Don't you believe in *making* a child go to church?" Miss Hopkins asked.

"I believe that children certainly ought to go to church as soon as they are old enough for it not be a punishment for them to keep still, and when the services are planned for children and young people as well as for adults," Mr. Newman replied. "Do you think that church might be made so pleasant that the children and young people will *want* to go? As Mrs. Gordon reminds us, when we were studying the way people learned we found that those things that pleased us and satisfied us were the things that we learned, and the things that we would keep on doing until they became habits. But we will never form the habit of doing a thing that does not please us in some way.

That is the reason why so many young people drop out of Sunday school; they have not found it to be a place that pleased them enough to cause them to keep on going after they reached the age when they were not 'taken' by some member of the family or were made to go by themselves. When we learn how to meet the needs of young people, to appeal to their wants or desires in the work of the Sunday school and Church, they will come of their own accord. But we have to know something about the needs and wants of children and young people, and of how their interests change as they grow, before we are able to satisfy their longings. We made a list of people's wants that we were talking about a few weeks ago. [See page 40.] Whenever you plan anything for the Sunday school or Church, you will be successful in your work if you see to it that it fills one or more of these wants."

"Well, I have heard that some people think that we should never *make* children do things, but let them do only what takes their fancy," said Mrs. Chapman. "It seems to me that this is a very weak sort of training. I believe that every one should do things that are hard and unpleasant merely because he *ought* to do them."

"You are certainly right, Mrs. Chapman, in thinking that it would not be right to avoid all the hard things in life," Mr. Newman answered. "Some of the things that we do may even be rather unpleasant themselves, but for

79

some reason we would not be satisfied unless we did them. Do you remember how Mrs. Sanders admitted that she would be willing to suffer or feel uncomfortable as a result of telling the truth, because she would feel even more uncomfortable and would suffer in her heart still more if she did not tell the truth? Now I venture that I can make one of the ladies in this group admit that washing the dishes 'pleases' her!"

"That is my regular job at home, but I surely do hate it. I get no pleasure from it, and I am not interested in doing it," Miss Hopkins challenged.

"If you feel that way about it, why don't you leave them unwashed until you use up all that are on the pantry shelf?" Mr. Newman asked.

"Nobody but a man would ever think of suggesting such a thing!" Miss Hopkins exclaimed. "Why, what would we think about ourselves and our home if we did not keep things neat and in order? No good housekeeper would consent to that."

"Your main or big interest is in being a good housekeeper, then," Mr. Newman said. "Now, in order to be pleased with yourself as a housekeeper, there are certain disagreeable things that you must do in order that your place may be clean and orderly. Therefore you do a thing that is really unpleasant in itself, so that you may get something else that you want very much—namely, a house that is sanitary and neat and that you can be proud of. When there are two things like that to choose between, you do the one that in the end will bring you more pleasure. Sometimes we do not stop to make a real choice, but do the thing because we have made a habit of doing it. Again, some things that we do because we *have* to do them may seem to be big tasks, but we do them for some purpose, and then we lose sight of the fact that *in them- selves* they are not really a pleasure. How many of you mothers have had to remind your girls to straighten their rooms each day?"

Some of the ladies smiled, and Mrs. Gordon spoke for the others: "Well, I suppose that every mother has had to do that more or less."

"However, you do not have to keep reminding your daughter to sweep her floor and dust the dresser on the day when the girls in her club are to meet in her home," Mr. Newman pointed out.

"My niece worked hard for two days making curtains for her room just before a friend came to visit her," Miss Hopkins said. "Her mother had bought the material for her a year before and had begged her again and again to hem the strips, but she did not seem to be interested in doing it until she was to have a guest."

"In thinking about why she did this we would say that she had her 'mind set' on making the room look pretty,

81

and therefore she was 'ready' to hem the curtains," Miss Bonner remarked. "Her longing for pretty things was not enough until she had another reason added to that one —namely, wanting to win the approval of her guest."

"As another case, let us think of a boy that has to carry stones out of a field that his father has just cleared," Mr. Newman suggested. "Does he find much pleasure in doing that?"

"I should say not!" Mr. Gordon said. "In fact, I had my thirteen-year-old son helping me in just that way recently, and could not understand why he was so cross about it and fooled around so much, when a few weeks before he had carried rocks bigger than those to build a fort with. When I asked him about it, he replied: 'Shucks, that was fun, because we boys were planning a game and had to have a fort for it.'"

"Yes," said Mr. Newman, "it is the purpose or aim that we have in mind that makes us do some more or less disagreeable things without fussing about it. We can sometimes help the children learn to do things in the home in such a way that they work with us instead of pulling against us. Of course we might simply *make* them do what we want them to do, but think how the other way saves time and effort and cross looks and words. Being forced to do a thing sometimes sets a person against it. I remember that when I was a little boy I was told that

I must learn to milk the cows, and I did learn in a fashion, but very unwillingly. I never could do it well or fast until a young cousin of mine came to visit us. He lived in the city, but he liked being on the farm and was always asking me how to do certain things. I taught him how to milk, and we used to race with the milking every morning. Of course I could not let him outdo me, and I worked so hard at it that I could soon do it even as fast as father could, and could strip the cow as well as he could, too."

"I suppose we could do a great deal more in leading our children to become interested in things like that if we just took the time for it," sighed Mrs. Sanders. "I am usually so busy that I could not stop to do anything like that very often. Yet now that I think about it, I may spend more time trying to make them keep on doing certain jobs than I would in helping them get started in the best way. Before hearing this discussion, I always thought that I had performed my duty by my children when I made them do what was right, but I realize that I was overlooking the most important part of all."

"If you did help them to want to do what they should do, Mrs. Sanders," Mr. Newman said, "their attitudes, or ways of acting and feeling, would probably be improved. You are really teaching a child, and he is learning, whenever you have anything whatsoever to do with him. We usually think of school as the place where our children

83

learn, but they probably learn as much on the playground or in their own homes as they do in the classroom. And no matter where they are or with whom they are, they are *learning,* all day long, week in and week out. When a person speaks harshly or acts rudely to a child, even if it be a stranger on the road, the child learns something from it and is building up attitudes toward everybody and everything that he has anything to do with."

"Do you think that after people are grown they ever learn things—very much, at least?" asked Miss Hopkins.

"I read a book about that recently," Miss Bonner said. "Some experiments have been carried on to see if adults could learn as well and as fast as girls and boys learn, and what was found out was very encouraging to me, since I have been teaching in day school for twenty-odd years, as you all know. In some few things that call for the use of muscles that children often use, but that we do not use much after we grow up, it was found that the children could do better. But in most things the adults could do just as well as the children. They could learn even more easily and quickly than the young folks could certain things that call for experience and for power to reason things out. And these people were put to learning all sorts of things, such as playing tennis and skating and throwing ball and drawing figures of certain shapes and

84

memorizing poetry and saying the alphabet backward and writing with the left hand."

"One reason why adults do not learn any more than they do is that they think they can't learn," Mr. Newman said. "Also they are really not very much interested in learning. The last few years I have known of a number of grandmothers who have gone to school, and they have done just about as good work as the young folks, which shows what older people can do when they really want to do it."

"I am sorry that it is time to leave," said Mrs. Ray, "because I should like to talk some more about how we can help our children to build attitudes, or ways of feeling and acting about things. I believe that, after all, that is the hardest part of teaching. It seems strange now that I never did think about this before, and also that I did not realize that pupils were learning all the time rather than just in the classroom. Perhaps we can talk about these things some other night."

CHAPTER VI

THEY WON'T KEEP STILL

"THE boys and girls in my class of juniors are so fidgety that I am about ready to give up. They will not keep still long enough to listen to what I try to tell them during the Sunday school hour," Miss Lane complained.

"We who have grown up do not have much trouble keeping still," Miss Bonner said. "In fact, some of us seem to be glad just to 'sit' and do nothing else. This is true partly because we are not growing as the children and young folks are. I have taught hundreds of children in the years I have been working in day school and Sunday school, and I have never yet seen a healthy child who could keep still any length of time. I used to try to make them keep still in school, and I scolded them because I had the idea that they were squirming just to annoy me. One day I was telling my troubles to an old aunt of mine who has reared a large family, and she warned me: 'The Lord made them so that they *can't* keep still. They have to be stirring all the time so that their little bodies can grow. Since they are going to be doing something all the time, the thing for you to do is to see to it that they are doing something worth while. I have reared nine of them, honey, and I know what I am talking about.' I began watching the children in a new way and read some books about them, and I learned a lot that has helped me. Since it is one of God's laws that they must be active in order to grow, when we try to *make* them keep still we are working against God's law instead of with it. Watch a tiny baby in his crib and notice how he waves his arms and kicks his legs, moving all the time unless he is asleep. Also he uses his lungs occasionally! Then as soon as he is able to crawl on the floor he is all over the house and into everything unless he is in a little coop. That is his way of taking the exercise that he needs for his muscles and bones. If you want to get an idea of perpetual motion, try to take care of a healthy child of four or five. Some experiments have been made with little children, and it was found that a child two or three years old can keep still only half a minute at a time, and a child from six to ten can keep still only a minute and a half."

"I have had so much trouble with the little tots in my beginner class that I have learned to keep them busy doing things, with only a few minutes at a time for the story or talk," said Mrs. Chapman. "But I have found that when they try to draw pictures or to help themselves by putting on their overshoes they can't manage very well. Can you tell me why that is so, Miss Bonner?"

"As their bodies grow," Miss Bonner answered, "the big muscles in their arms and legs develop first. You will find that a baby can play better with a fairly large ball than with a tiny one, not to mention the fact that if the ball is very small it will be in his mouth before you know what has happened. When they are only four or five years old they cannot use the little muscles in their fingers so well as they can a few years later. Even when they start to school they have trouble trying to write small letters, and the words usually sprawl all over the page. However, they learn quickly and soon manage a pencil pretty well."

"What you said about why children are so active has helped me with my problem," Miss Lane said. "My class worry me with their squirming, but I believe that I shall be able to put up with it better now, and I shall try to keep them busy doing things."

"Well, you may think that you are having a hard time with your class, but you could not have more trouble than I am having with my girls of fourteen and fifteen," said Mrs. Gordon. "Did you learn anything about why the pupils of that age are so hard to manage, Miss Bonner?"

"In the teen years the boys and girls are growing rapidly, as all parents know, for this is the time when the dresses have to be lengthened and new suits have to be bought," Miss Bonner replied. "They have times of rapid growth and times of slow growth until their bodies are mature. During the periods of slow growth the different parts of the body are developing, trying to catch up with each other and to work together well in spite of the change in size. In the teen age, too, the bones and muscles do not always grow at the same rate. When the bones grow faster, this pulls the muscles. When the muscles grow faster, this crowds them on the bones."

"Does that fast growing have anything to do with making the boys clumsy?" asked Miss Hopkins. "My nephew is the most awkward person imaginable. The other night at the supper table he asked for the butter. When he reached out to take the plate, he knocked off the knife, and as he tried to pick it up he turned over his glass of water. And he was so ashamed of his awkwardness that I felt sorry for him and told his mother to stop scolding him."

"The boys and girls of that age need some friends who understand," said Mr. Newman. "They are having trouble because their limbs are lengthening so fast that they can't measure distance as they used to. Suppose that everything you reached for was an inch or so closer to you than you thought. Would you have any trouble handling things? That is practically what has happened to these boys and girls. They have not been able to realize that their arms and legs are longer than they were, and so they miscalculate and turn things over and drop things,

89

through no fault of their own, but because they have new bodies to take care of and have not learned how to do it yet. One great difficulty about their awkwardness is that it embarrasses them very much. They become nervous about how they will enter a room and how they will meet people. This makes them even more liable to stumble over nothing at all. Their feet seem to get in their way. And added to this, when the boy's voice is changing, he begins a sentence in a low tone and ends up with a funny little squeak which startles him as much as it does us."

"I believe their dispositions and ideas at this age are just as uncertain as their voices and their movements," said Mrs. Gordon. "They are moody and change their opinions about a thing before you know what has happened. They are gay and light-hearted one day and so gloomy the next that one can hardly live with them."

"I wish we could always remember that while we have trouble with these adolescents they are having much more trouble with themselves and are much more concerned about it all!" Mr. Newman exclaimed. "They do not understand what is the matter and cannot depend upon themselves. All these changes in feeling are in large part the result of real changes that are taking place in their bodies. There are certain glands in the body that give out liquids. Some of these glands you are familiar with, such as the tear gland and the sweat glands. Others lie deep within the body and do not give out any fluid that you see. The fluid goes into the blood and brings about certain important changes in it. The sex glands give out a liquid externally as well as another kind that goes into the body. These sex glands are very active at this time, as they have matured and can operate properly. It is necessary, by the way, to see that boys and girls of this age know the main facts about sex. They are going to learn them in some way, and it is very unfortunate for them to learn from people that do not feel as they should about sex or who are ignorant as to what should be told to young folks. Of course parents should not wait until their children are in the teens to begin explaining to them the meaning of sex. The first simple statements about it should be made when the little child asks questions as to where he came from, and the father and the mother are the ones to tell their children. It is dangerous to wait too long to do this. If the parents do not know what to say, they can get some good books on sex education."

"I should like to get the names of the books you refer to," Mr. Morris put in. "I told my wife recently that I was going to ask you for some literature on this subject. I need some books and leaflets to put in the hands of the fathers and mothers who realize the importance of sex education, but who are uncertain as to what they should say to their boys and girls. I am pleased that you mentioned this." [See page 171 for a list of these books.]

"I am glad to learn some facts about the physical development of children and young people," Mr. Gordon said. "Please tell us more about it."

"Some of the glands that I spoke of before are responsible for how tall we grow and how nervous we are, and trouble comes if they give out either too much or too little liquid," Mr. Newman explained. "Along with the growth of the glands, there is the growth of the body and its organs. The heart and the lungs grow at a different rate, and sometimes the body has difficulty in working as it should. For example, the frame of the body itself grows faster than the heart in some years, and again the heart grows faster than the arteries. At the same time the muscles need exercise, and this causes the boys and girls to be very active and boisterous. However, the heart cannot supply the blood fast enough, and this makes children tire easily. They play hard for a while and then stop suddenly. After resting for a while they jump up unexpectedly and are off doing something else. Now, some boys and girls are inclined to be lazy at times, and that should not be encouraged. However, we who have to work with them, we teachers and parents, should be very sure that they are not 'ailing' before we accuse them of laziness. Quite often a child is cross or disobedient because he is not well or because there are certain changes taking place in his body that he does not understand—in fact, that he knows nothing about. So we should study the children and learn all that we can about them in order that we may be just to them and not expect too much of them when they are not physically able to keep on with either work or play."

"I was interested in what you said about boys in the teens being active. I know this from experience. They surely do act like wild Indians!" Mrs. Ray exclaimed.

"Knowing these things about boys and girls does not mean that you will be able to change them, for they are just growing up as God intends for them to grow," Mr. Newman said. "But the knowledge certainly should make us more patient. James and Ed will still race through the house and gallop down the steps like a team of horses and yell at the top of their voices, but we can stand the racket and confusion better when we know why they act as they do. For example, they seem to yell just for the fun of it. They do not know that their lungs are developing and need exercise, and that whistling and shouting help the lungs grow and ward off disease. The boys just make the noise, and the old folks suffer from it. And we must be willing to put up with it, though the boys should learn to be considerate and to get out in the fields to do most of their shouting instead of doing it in the house."

"My sister thinks that her adolescent boy is a little savage because he is awkward and noisy," Miss Hopkins said, "and she says that he will never be civilized. She will be encouraged when I tell her what I have heard to-night."

"I am troubled about my girl because she is just thirteen years old, and yet she is taller than most of the boys her age. I have often said jokingly that I'd have to put a brick on her head, for she will be a giant if she keeps on growing at this rate," said Mrs. Ray.

"You need not be worried about that," Miss Bonner reassured her. "At that age almost all girls grow faster than boys, and weigh more than the boys do, too. The boys are in a period of slow growth. It is strange how growth comes in 'waves,' as I said before. First there is a very rapid growth in infancy. Then comes a slowing up at about six. This is followed by a new spurt around eight years of age, with another slowing up before the teens are reached. In adolescence both boys and girls seem to shoot up overnight. Girls of twelve or thirteen grow more rapidly than boys of the same age, but they will slow up a bit later on, and the boys will not only catch up with them, but will outstrip them. You know that, as a rule, men are taller than women, and yet when these women were girls of thirteen or fourteen they were probably taller than the boys of their age."

"You said something awhile ago about children playing and romping," Mrs. Sanders said. "Don't you think that they should be allowed to play a great deal?"

"If they do not play, they will never get the exercise that they need," Miss Bonner said. "We sometimes think of play as being more or less foolish and unnecessary, but a wise God made children active so that they would grow. Since it is a law of nature that children be active, it is our job to see that they are active in the right way, and play is a mighty fine form of activity. You can get exercise through work, but the exercise is not half so good if you are not enjoying it. Being easy and free in what you do, simply doing things for the joy and amusement in them and not being bound to do certain things when you do not want to do them, is what every boy and girl has a right to for a great part of the time. Some home duties should be carried out by every child, according to his age and strength, and some of their tasks in the home can be made to seem like games, but much free play is every child's right. The Church has a decided responsibility to see that the children have a place to play and that the right kind of play is made possible. In large cities it has been found that the number of crimes in certain districts was reduced an amazing degree when the children were provided with playgrounds. Boys and girls are going to have fun in some way, and we want them to have the kind of fun that will help them instead of the kind that tends to make them crooks and good-for-nothing folks. Do you know any good things that children learn from playing together?"

"Well, we have been talking about the need of exercise for the body, so that is the first thing," said Miss Hopkins. "I think another good point is that other children will keep a child from being too selfish. My nephew was badly spoiled at home, and every one gave in to him, but when he spent two months in the home of his cousins he found that they would not put up with his selfish ways. He had to take his turn and share with the others, or his playmates would not have anything to do with him. This helped him, and it was easier to get along with him when he came back home. All of the family noticed the change and decided to take advantage of it and to help him learn to share with those in his home."

"A child learns to be a good sport when he plays with other children, too," Miss Lane suggested. "I knew a girl who pouted and sulked when she did not get her own way, and when she went to school and began playing in the yard there the others in her class would not choose her for either side in their games, so that she was left out until she changed her way of behaving. Also I knew a boy who cheated in games and was put out of his gang until he promised not to do it again."

"I agree with you about these things," Mr. Chester remarked, "but when we were talking about sex education I was thinking of the danger of boys and girls becoming too curious about sex, perhaps even to the extent of being indiscreet.

"You are right, Mr. Chester," Mr. Newman said. "Children should not only be acquainted with facts about sex, but they should not have too much temptation put in their way. A wise parent will look after his children and will also talk frankly with them. An air of mystery and a 'hushing up' when questions are asked will arouse curiosity and lead the children to want to find out what it is all about."

"Another danger about play is that boys sometimes become bullies when they are with children who are younger or smaller than themselves," said Mrs. Ray. "When a boy becomes a bully, this bad habit may stay with him when he is a man. Some fathers that I know pride themselves on being good at disciplining their children when I believe that they are really just working off their desire to bully weaker persons. I am always doubtful about a man who boasts that he makes his children do what he tells them to do without ever talking over with them the reasons why they should do these things."

"I believe that one of the chief values of play is that in a team boys and girls learn to work for the good of the group and not for selfish reasons," Mr. Morris said. "A boy who makes a sacrifice hit or a girl who does not protest when a substitute takes her place on the basket ball team has developed certain qualities that are needed for citizenship in the community and also in the Kingdom. I wish there were more adults who had this sporting spirit and this willingness to give up desirable things for the sake of the group."

"Play has many other good features," Mr. Newman pointed out. "In play, children are quick in their actions and also in their thinking. They have to be accurate, for when they are careless about counting up their points in a ball game or moving their men on a pachisi board their partners or opponents will check up on them. And the lessons that are learned through their being with other children are taken to heart much more than the lessons we try to teach them by lecturing or scolding them in the classroom or in the home. On the playground the boys and girls are *living*. Their experiences there are natural, and they learn that if they disobey certain rules punishment is sure to come. The punishment that children get at home is often something that has little connection with what they have done. A child may be spanked whenever he does anything that displeases

98

his mother or father. But the child may connect the parent with the spanking rather than connecting the punishment with the various things that he has done. On the playground a girl who sulks is left out of the game, and a boy who cheats is not allowed in the gang. Now, these are what I call 'natural punishments' in the sense that a child understands clearly that what he has done brings about the punishment that his playmates deal out to him."

"There is so much value in play that I think we ought to pay more attention to the recreation that our pupils have. I believe that we could fix up some place here in town for the boys and girls in our Sunday school to use as a playground," Mr. Gordon suggested. "A few of us could clear off the small trees in the lot two doors from the church and buy some equipment. Perhaps if we could arrange for basket ball and tennis matches and also for some other games in both winter and summer, the young folks would not spend so much time as they do in automobiles or in loafing in the drug store. I am very much troubled about what they do with their free hours, and I believe this plan would help us solve the problem."

"That is an excellent idea," Miss Hopkins said, "and it would not be so expensive as you might think. I have a friend in another town who has provided a playground for her boys and for many of the other children in the neighborhood without spending much money. She says that she thinks the children of rich people are often much less satisfied in their play than those of poor people, for they have ready-made equipment and elaborate toys that cannot be tinkered with. This mother has turned her back yard into a playground, and the boys can use it as they please. They have a few carpenter's tools, and when they hear of a house being built they ask permission of the workmen to pick up blocks and pieces of lumber that have been thrown aside. With these scraps of wood and with old boxes that they find, the boys have a chance to make sheds and rough furniture and other things. Doing this keeps them occupied and happy. They dig holes in the ground, and they make radio sets and trains. Once they even built a little town with roads and houses and filling stations and stores. Also they play basketball and baseball and football, and all the boys in the neighborhood are eager to be allowed to play with them. On rainy days their mother puts some cardboard over her dining room table, and they play ping-pong in the dining room. She says that she values her boys more than she does her belongings, and she is always ready to play with them as well as to help them plan games with other children. Recently she was talking with some mothers who were much troubled because their children went to so many picture shows that were not the kind that they ought to see. This woman said that she had never faced that problem, because her boys were always so busy that they rarely found time to go to picture shows."

"Suppose we close our discussion for the evening, Mr. Newman," Mr. Morris suggested, "and choose a committee now to make arrangements for a place where our pupils may play. If we do not get a start now, we are apt to let our interest cool off and do nothing about it."

The other members of the group agreed, and they were soon talking with enthusiasm about games and equipment and plans for a playground.

CHAPTER VII

WHY ARE THEY SO DIFFERENT?

"Why is it that often people in the same family are quite different from each other?" asked Mr. Gordon. "I have thought about this a lot since two young nephews of mine, my brother's boys, have come to visit in our home recently. You know that our Thomas is very fond of having a good time and running around with the other young folks, and we thought that both of my nephews would join him, since one is only a year older than Thomas is, and the other is a year younger. Edward, the elder of the two, is just like his father, always ready for a lark and the life of any party that he goes to. But Howard is shy and quiet and does not mix well with the other boys and girls. He prefers to get a book and go off into a corner to read it, or to wander around the farm, or to go fishing with me. Ed has come to see us often, but this is the first time that Howard has made us a visit for some years. The difference between them seems to be more noticeable each year, though they have the same parents and live in the same home."

"Well, it is easy enough to see that persons inherit looks or size from some member of the family," Mr. Newman replied. "For instance, your Thomas is just like you, 'a chip off the old block,' as I have heard your friends tell you. And you say that Edward is like his father. Is Howard like his mother?"

"No," Mr. Gordon answered, "that is the strange thing about it. He is not like any of the family that I know, though his mother says that she remembers an old aunt who was quiet and used to read a great deal. Perhaps he 'favors' her."

"When we think about what we have inherited from our families, we must remember that there are a great many people from whom our inheritance comes," Mr. Newman said. "A child has two parents, four grandparents, eight great-grandparents, sixteen great-great-grandparents, and so on, back farther than we can count. A child may be like his father or his mother, or like each of them in certain ways—a sort of mixture. Or he may be like one of his sixteen great-great-grandparents, or inherit certain looks or 'ways' from a number of his ancestors. When you consider all the possible inheritances of children, it really seems strange that we do not find them more unlike than they are."

"Why is it that there are sometimes twins that are exactly alike?" asked Mrs. Chapman.

"In the many years that I have been teaching in Sunday school and day school I have had a number of sets of twins in my classes," Miss Bonner put in. "At first I thought they would be exactly the same, particularly when they looked so much alike that for some weeks I could not tell them apart, but when I learned to know them well I found that in most cases there were very decided differences. However, there are 'identical' twins every now and then—those that are so much alike that you always have a hard time telling them apart. They are alike not only in looks, but in some ways of acting and thinking and feeling. As they grow older, it is probable that they will become less and less alike. Those who have studied the human body are able to tell us why there are identical twins, but such cases are rare. In my opinion, we should be interested chiefly in the differences between people, for we are too apt to treat our pupils as though they were all alike."

"With so many ancestors and so many traits that may be inherited from one or a number of those ancestors, we can account for both the differences and the likenesses in families," said Mr. Newman. "Sometimes you find a couple that seem to be different in most respects, just as Mr. and Mrs. Gordon are. They bring to their children the possibility of being like themselves or like their ancestors on either side of the family, as I have said before. When a child does not resemble any member of the family that is now living, he probably resembles some ancestor far back, and may seem very different from all the other children in his own family and also from his cousins. After all, there are no two children that inherit *exactly* the same things; and, as I said before, this is not strange when you think about how many possible mixtures or combinations there may be of the ways and looks of people from so many lines."

"In my Sunday school class I have a boy and a girl who are twins. They are as different in their ways of acting as day and night, but I suppose that is chiefly because one is a boy and the other is a girl," said Miss Hopkins. "It is surprising to see how very much like each other they look, but they are not alike in any other way."

"How are they different?" Miss Bonner asked.

"Well, the girl is neat and prim and is very careful about having her lessons just right each day. She is quiet and timid, but you can rely on her absolutely. On the other hand, the boy is boisterous and loud and is always taking the lead in things, especially in out-of-door games," Miss Hopkins answered.

"I have a girl in my class who is very much like the boy you describe, and I know a boy who is as quiet and timid as that girl," Miss Bonner said. "There must be some reason besides sex to make the difference. What can you tell us about the children, Mr. Newman?"

"We are in the habit of thinking about boys as acting

and feeling in certain ways and about girls as acting and feeling in ways different from the boys," Mr. Newman answered. "However, can any of you mention anything that a boy does that you have not known at least a few girls to do, or the other way around?"

"A girl can't really throw a ball well," Mrs. Sanders volunteered.

"I have a niece who can, but I disapprove heartily of her being such a tomboy as she is," said Mr. Brown. "She is about the only girl that I have ever known who could hit a barn door, and I must confess that I admire her skill in throwing, even though I do not think her mother ought to let her play ball with the boys."

"The shoulder of a girl is not actually different from the shoulder of a boy," Mr. Newman explained, "and it is rather her lack of training and practice that makes it difficult for her to throw a ball. Can any of you tell me real differences between girls and boys?" Mr. Newman asked.

There was a pause while the members of the group tried to find an answer to this question. Finally one of them said: "I am sure that we should be able to think of numbers of things, but every time I believe I have thought of a trait that only girls have I remember some boy whom I know or have heard of who has that same trait. Will you tell us the reason for this, Mr. Newman?"

He smiled and answered: "I believe that one of the chief reasons why girls are somewhat different from boys is the one that Mr. Brown expressed so vehemently— namely, that we expect certain things of girls and do not expect other things, and that in most cases the girls have lived up to our ideas of what they should do. How often did you ladies hear your mothers say to you when you were girls, 'That is not laᴅyᴸᵢᵏᵉ, my dear,' or 'Nice little girls don't do that'? And about the worst thing that a boy could be accused of was being a 'sissy.' He could not bear to have anyone think that he was like a girl in any way. And so there have been built up many ideas of what the two sexes should do, and finally people began to think that boys and girls were *born* very different. There are some ways in which they really are different, as has been found out from experiments. Boys have more strength and can move more rapidly. They are more interested in things such as machinery and the way it works, and they tire less easily than girls. On the other hand, girls are more interested in people, more likely to be ruled by their feelings, and more inclined to nurse and comfort living things. And girls are less inclined than boys to take part in sports. But even in these things there are as great differences between some girls and other girls as there are between *girls* and *boys*. There are some other minor ways in which boys are unlike girls, but the amazing thing

107

is that there are not such great differences as we think before we really stop to study how boys and girls feel and act. The fact of sex is only one cause, and not a very prominent one, of the differences between men and women. Certainly a more important reason is the one I have just mentioned, that from the time they are little children there are certain things expected of them because of their sex, and they try to live up to those expectations. Training throughout childhood and youth probably has more to do with the differences than the fact that one is a boy and one is a girl."

"When I was a boy I never did think that a girl could do anything, but I have found out that a lot of them can do most of the things boys do and can do them just as well," Mr. Brown remarked. "One thing about young people to-day that I like very much is that they are more frank and open with each other than they used to be. I certainly believe in teaching the boys and girls to be polite to each other and to respect each other, even when they are in the same family."

"I think you are right, Mr. Brown," Miss Hopkins put in. "I have a sister who has reared all of her children to have genuine respect for each other, and I notice the difference between them and other young people. Such training should be given in the home. When this is done, their respect for each other carries young folks over many rough and dangerous places."

"Talking about respect for other people makes me think of how I believe we ought to act toward other races," said Mr. Chester. "All of us would do well to think of how Jesus acted toward the people of every race with which he had anything to do. The Golden Rule should work here, I believe."

"Yes," said Mr. Newman, "and, after all, there are not such great differences between races as we sometimes think. We are chiefly interested in how folks look and the funny little ways that they have, and forget to think of how they feel and think. A great many of the differences are caused by the fact that they do not have the same customs and clothes and language that we have. If a tiny Chinese baby were brought over here and reared in an American home, he would dress and talk and act just as we do. Of course the first thing that we should notice would be the color of his skin and the slant of his eyes, and that would make us feel that he was different. But he could probably do as well in school as our children do, and would think and talk about the same things and play games just as our boys and girls do. We do not try to understand all that is going on behind the things that we can actually see."

109

"I had a friend who lived in New York, where there are lots of children whose parents are foreigners," Miss Bonner said. "She told me that if you would stay with the boys and girls in her class, with your eyes closed, you could hardly tell whether you were in their classroom or in the classroom of the children of native American parents. And most of them look very much like us because they dress as we do."

"While all of you have been talking," said Miss Lane, "I have been thinking about one thing that I can't understand. I have a niece who used to be pleased to meet new people, was always eager to study, and was unusually obedient. But she is sixteen years old now, and she has certainly changed in every one of those ways. She is shy about going out to parties, she spends lots of her time reading books and neglects her school work, and her mother says she has a time getting her to do things that she used to be ready to do without being told. She is surely different from what she used to be. What made her change like that?"

"You remember we were talking last week about the changes that take place when boys and girls are thirteen and fourteen years old," said Mr. Newman. "The changes that we notice and that we can see are signs of even greater changes that are taking place within them,

110

but which we cannot see. It is simply natural for boys and girls at this age to change as your niece has, because they are growing up. You know growth brings about great changes in the way they look—in their size, often in the color of their hair, and in other ways. From the time that a person is a baby until he is a grown man and even until he dies, he is always changing. A child is not interested in the things that young folks are interested in. A baby will play with a ball, simply handling it and turning it over and dropping it. A boy of eight will want to pitch it or throw it against the side of the house and then catch it. A sixteen-year-old boy must play a game of baseball with all the rules that teams must follow. A man may play occasionally, or may like to pitch ball with his children, but he usually prefers to go to the ball field and watch a game. So our desires and wants change their form throughout life. We are very apt to think of ourselves—of what *we* can do and how *we* feel and what *we* want—and expect others to do and feel and want the same things. We do not know how we were when we were babies. We forget how we were when we were children. We even do not have patience with the ways of the young folks, because we are 'set' in our own ways. It is a fine thing that we can and do change, for the world would be a sorry place if we did not. The fact that we are always changing may work either of two ways, for good or evil.

111

As Sunday school workers we are very much interested that the right kind of change will take place—that our boys and girls will be finer and finer as the years go by. If the changes are not for good, they will be for evil. Thieves, crooks, criminals of all sorts did not become so overnight. When they were born they had the chance to go in either direction. The 'divine spark' that is in each of us at birth must be carefully watched and tended in order that each one may 'grow in grace' and develop as God intended that he should. Jesus had a deep belief in the possibilities of little children, as he showed when he said that older persons who would enter the Kingdom must 'become as little children.' "

"It certainly places a great responsibility on teachers in the Sunday school to know that they must help guide the boys and girls as they grow," Miss Hopkins said. "My chief trouble is that when I find a good way of working with a boy I think that I can use that same way with some other boy. But it never does work out exactly as I think it will. Is it the fault of the children, or is the fault mine?"

"In my work," Miss Bonner said, "I have found that exactly the same plan will not work with two boys, not because the plan is not right, but because the boys are so different. You know in your flower garden there are never two flowers that are exactly alike. So it is with children. There are never two that are exactly the same, and most of them are very, very different. Yet we are in the habit of treating them as though they were just alike, and that gets us into trouble. Not only is each boy different from every other boy, but the same boy cannot be treated in the same way when he is a child and when he is thirteen or fourteen years old."

"It always helps me to make a list of the points that we take up in our discussion," Miss Lane said. "Suppose we work out one now."

The others agreed, and the following items were listed as the reasons why people are different from each other:

> *Inheritance.*—From parents, grandparents, and other ancestors. This is probably the chief reason.
>
> *Race.*—This causes such slight differences that it is difficult to say what they are.
>
> *Sex.*—Most of the differences that we notice between men and women have been brought about because of their training and environment.
>
> *Age.*—Not only are people of different ages different, but the same person changes from year to year.

"Now, that will help me keep in mind what we have talked about to-night," Miss Lane said. "However, I am not at all certain what it is that people inherit from

113

their ancestors. If a man is a carpenter, will his children be more apt to be good carpenters than they would be if he did not have that trade?"

"I cannot answer your question," Mrs. Ray said, "but I do know that not only carpentering but also such things as loving music and being able to teach seem to run in the same family. Can you tell us why that is, Mr. Newman?"

"It is true that trades or professions do 'run in the family' quite frequently," Mr. Newman replied, "but that does not mean that the children have come into the world ready and able to enter these trades or professions. A child whose parents are very smart has many times more chances to be smart than a child whose parents are dull. He inherits a general 'smartness' or ability to do things well, but exactly what he will do is determined by his surroundings, in most cases. The son of a brilliant lawyer may be a brilliant lawyer himself, but it is probable that if he were a teacher or a doctor he would be just as brilliant in one of these professions as in law. The amount of intelligence that we have is something that we get from our family, but what we do with it is usually a result of our surroundings. Both my father and uncle were school-teachers. As far back as I can remember I heard them talk about school and new ideas in education and how important education is until it seemed to me that preparing to be a teacher was the most natural thing in the world, and I rather took it for granted that I should take normal work. If my parents had died when I was a baby and I had been sent to live in the home of a business man where I heard business discussed all the time, it is probable that I would have gone into the business world. Many boys take up farming because they have been reared on farms. It is the same way with weaving and bricklaying and working in stores. However, there is more chance now for young people to get out into the world and find out about various kinds of work than there was when I was a boy. More girls and boys go to college now than did when I was young, and there is less reason for them to carry on their fathers' occupations."

"I see what you mean about how one's surroundings play a large part in what work one decides to take up," Miss Lane said, "but what about inheriting temper or laziness or forgetfulness of names? I have noticed that these traits are very common in families."

"I believe that being high-tempered may be inherited in part," Miss Bonner said, "but I knew an interesting case once. One of my pupils used to have very bad attacks of temper, and we excused her on the ground that she was just like her mother. Her mother died, and this child went to live with a sweet old aunt who was remarkable in controlling herself. In a year's time this child was so different that one would hardly have recognized her. That changed my ideas considerably."

"People do inherit different kinds of nervous systems, and that tends to make them more or less apt to 'fly off,'" Mr. Newman added, "but a great deal of the bad temper in the world has been *learned*. This is true about many other things, such as being orderly or being happy; in fact, having a good disposition in general is in part the result of learning. The training begins early in life, really when the child is a wee baby. Many children go into a rage because they find that in this way they can get what they want. As we discovered when we were talking about learning, a person repeats those things that bring him satisfaction."

"Well, I had always thought before that one had to accept children more or less as one found them," Mrs. Sanders said. "I have often heard a mother sighing, 'What can I expect of Dan when his grandfather and father were just that way?' We can lead children to change their dispositions to a large extent, but I don't suppose they can change in every way."

"That is true," Mr. Newman said, "but as teachers who are trying to lead children and young people into the 'more abundant life' that Jesus wants all of us to have, we can be encouraged by the fact that changes do take place, and we must do all we can to have those changes of the right sort. We probably cannot change the amount of intelligence that a child has, but we can see to it that he has a chance to use what intelligence he has in the best way possible."

"I think I understand what you are trying to get us to see," Mrs. Gordon said. "Children have inherited certain things from their parents, and there is no way to change the fact of this inheritance. On the other hand, we must take the children as they are and help them as much as we can. I have heard a number of people argue as to which is more important, inheritance or environment, some emphasizing one and some the other. But as I see it, we teachers are interested in what our pupils have inherited because the more we know about this, the better we understand them. Our chief interest should probably be the surroundings of the children and young people, for we do have a chance to change the environment to some extent at least."

"Yes, that is what I had in mind in large part," Mr. Newman said. "For example, we are concerned about the character of a certain person in our Sunday school class. Now, his character is a result of what he was when he was born plus what has happened to him since his birth. When he was born he had a certain kind of body, a certain physical make-up, and also a 'leaning toward' certain traits. We speak of these 'leanings' as tendencies. But how these tendencies were developed, whether certain

117

ones grew stronger or weaker, depended greatly on what surroundings the baby grew up in and how his parents and teachers trained him. My mother was very wise when she said that men and women should be concerned chiefly with heredity when they are deciding whom they should marry. Since the inheritance of their children is very important, they should think of what they will pass on to them. But after the children are born, the parents should put all their emphasis on environment, on how they will rear them. So we see that children who have different tendencies or 'leanings' should be treated in different ways, even though they are members of the same family. To do our best work as teachers we must know the parents of our pupils and their home life and the attitudes that their families have toward them. Then we must try to bring about certain changes that are needed, encouraging one tendency and discouraging another. Let us see what we can find out about the heredity and environment of our pupils by the middle of next week, when we will meet again."

CHAPTER VIII

HOW DO THEY FEEL ABOUT THINGS?

"I HAVE often decided that I would give up my Sunday school class," Mrs. Chapman said, "but I have never come to the point of resigning, because I feel that it would not be a Christian thing to do. One should have a part in the work of the Church; and as I know how to teach better than anything else I do, I just feel that I ought to keep at it, even though it is hard for me to come every Sunday."

"Are there women in the Church who would make good teachers, but who will not take a class?" Mr. Newman asked.

"I should say so!" Mrs. Chapman answered. "I was talking with Mrs. Graham about this only the other day, and she said that she knew she ought to teach, since she had been to normal school and had some courses in principles of teaching, but she felt it would be too much on her, and she could not decide to take that class of young people that needs a teacher so badly."

"Does how you *feel* about a thing determine what you are going to *do* about it?" Mr. Newman asked.

"I suppose so," Mrs. Chapman said. "If I did not feel that I ought to keep my class, I'd give it up, as I have just said. I believe there are lots of people who know they

119

ought to do things for the Church, but that does not seem to be enough to move them and lead them to do the things that are needed. It is the same way with me about some things. For instance, I know that I should go to see a certain old lady who is sick, but I confess that I must not feel strongly enough about it, for I have kept on putting off going to see her ever since I had word two weeks ago about her illness."

"If a member of your family became ill, and you had news of it, do you think that you would put off going to see *her?*" asked Mr. Newman.

"I would go as fast as I could get there," Mrs. Chapman answered. "If one whom you love is ill or is in trouble, you cannot reach her quickly enough."

"That is because your feelings have been aroused," Mr. Newman said. "A feeling is something very strong, and we call it an 'emotion,' which really means a 'stirred-up feeling inside.' Merely knowing a thing is not enough. You must have a feeling about it that is strong enough to lead you to act. If Mrs. Graham loved children or Church work enough, she would have taken a class in Sunday school long ago; but you have not been able to persuade her to teach, even though she says she realizes that she ought to do it. Is there any way of *making* her feel as you want her to feel?"

"I should certainly like to find it out if there is such

a way," Mr. Brown put in. "It seems as though we ought to be able to persuade her, but none of us has had any success as yet in arguing with her."

"I believe that it is not possible to *make* her feel differently," Mr. Newman said. "You might help her become acquainted with some of the young people in the class. Then when you saw that she was very much interested in them you might suggest to her that the class needs a good teacher, and she might be willing to take it. But no amount of mere arguing will have very much effect upon her. This is true about other people, too. Do we always think of this when we are working with our pupils?"

"I am sure that I have not," said Miss Hopkins. "I have argued with my class, telling them that they ought to love the Church and that they ought to have respect for older people, and so forth, but I have not been able to do very much toward making them feel as I want them to. If you can't *make* children feel a certain way, what *can* you do?"

"It is a question that has been studied a good deal, and one that is still hard to answer," Mr. Newman said. "Perhaps we can understand it better if we consider what has been found out about the emotions, those feelings of being upset all over. A certain man who has worked a great deal with children says that when babies are born they

121

have three emotions—fear, anger, and love. It is strange that they have so few at birth, when we think of how many they have later on. And it is still stranger to think that the babies show these emotions only when certain things happen to them. They are afraid of a loud noise and of falling. They are angry only when they are held so that they cannot move around easily. They show love or pleasure when they are made comfortable."

"Do you mean that a baby does not become angry except when it is held too tightly?" asked Mrs. Chapman. "I know that my children used to be very angry when they were hungry. They would scream until they were given something to eat."

"The amount of crying that a baby does even when it is hungry depends largely on habit," Mr. Newman replied. "By the time a child is a few months old he has learned all sorts of tricks and is able to make people do many things that he wants them to do. I have been talking about babies only a few days old. Now let us take one of those emotions and see how it grows and changes. Whenever you dress a baby or put on his coat or wrap, you have to hold him rather tightly, and you try to keep him from waving his arms or putting his fingers in his mouth while you are putting his arms into the sleeves of the coat. Now, the baby does not like to be held in that way, and he shows you so by screaming and kicking.

Soon he comes to know that a coat means being held against his will, and he fusses at the sight of it. He does not stop to reason it out, but he has learned that the coat and being held go together, and he has formed the habit of crying when he sees the coat. Again, you usually hold a baby in an uncomfortable position when you wash his ears. You should be very careful and as gentle as possible in handling the baby, because at best it is hard on the little fellow. Later on the child is kept from doing certain things that he wants to do, such as writing on the walls, or breaking up a box, or going fishing with the gang. If you want to find out how many times you tell your child not to do things that he wants to do, you should count up how often you say 'Don't . . .' Then remember that each one of these 'don'ts' means that the child is not allowed to follow his natural wants and interests. It is just another way of 'holding him tightly,' and each time it happens he rebels more or less, whether he shows it or not. So it goes on and on. He is made angry about one thing and then another, until there is a long list of things that 'make him mad,' as he says. He *learns* to be angry about these things. When he was a baby he became angry only when he was held too closely."

"Well, however it is with anger, I know that I was born with a fear of snakes and of mice," Miss Hopkins insisted.

123

"You begin learning things as soon as you are born, and it is hard to tell whether you have learned something or had it at birth," Mr. Newman explained. "For many years we have rather expected girls and women to be afraid of mice, and it may be that you are just trying to live up to these expectations. I know a man who said that one day he was in his garden with his little girl when she saw a snake for the first time in her life. She put out her hand to touch it, but he pulled her back and told her never to do that. Later on she saw another snake, and she began crying loudly and ran to her father in much fear. She had learned to be afraid of snakes because her father had shown her that he was afraid for her to touch one. So she will probably become more and more afraid of them as time goes on. Experiences of this sort have an effect on children that they rarely get away from even when they grow up. And one of the most serious things about it is that the fear of one thing may be carried over to other things until there is a whole collection of fears springing from the first one. You remember what I told you some weeks ago about Peter and his rabbit. In the same way the little girl who saw the snake in the garden might finally come to the point where she would be afraid of the garden itself. Another example is a child who has learned to be afraid of the dark. He was not born that way. He is probably spoiled by having a light in his room

124

when he is put to bed, and he finally becomes afraid if the light is put out and he is left alone in the dark. Suppose also that one night he falls out of the bed in the dark and wakes up and finds that there is no light in the room. He may then think of the darkness and the fall together. To scold a child about being afraid of the dark will not help him overcome the fear. Reading a poem to him such as John Martin's 'The Friendly Dark' or playing with him a game of finding a toy or book in a dark room will lead him to dread the night less."

"I am going to try out that plan with my little boy," Mr. Morris said. "Can any other members of the group suggest a way in which we can help our own children or our pupils get rid of another fear?"

"While Mr. Newman was talking, I was thinking of an experience I had with my first child," Mrs. Gordon said. "I used to be terribly frightened by a thunderstorm, and whenever the lightning would flash I would run to Elizabeth and grab her up and hold her close while I complained about the storm. In doing this I was actually teaching her to be afraid of a storm. When she was about five years old she came running in from the yard one day and threw herself in my lap and gasped: 'O, I see a big black cloud in the sky, and I am sure there will be a storm!' I shall never forget the look of terror on the child's face and how I felt when I realized that she

125

feared a storm even more than I did. I determined right then to help her to overcome this terror, so I held her quietly in my arms and told her that nothing would harm her. I said that the thunder was the sound of the cloud-soldiers attacking in battle and that the lightning was the flash of their swords as they fought. 'There is the first flash now,' I exclaimed as a bolt of lightning cut across the dark clouds. 'That is the leader drawing his sword, and the noise of the rain is really the rush of the feet of the soldiers.' I was working hard to keep from trembling myself as I talked to her, but I was rewarded by seeing her raise her head and open one eye. 'There must be a lot of soldiers fighting to make so much noise,' she commented as the rain poured down. Then she ducked her head again at the next flash. By the end of the summer, after she had seen a number of storms, she would come into the room with me when the thunder began to roll, but she could watch the skies and talk about the 'battle in the heavens' without the terror that distressed me so much on that spring day I spoke of. And the strangest thing about it was the fact that I became less afraid of storms myself, since I had to act so often as though I was not afraid."

"I had an experience something like that one summer years ago when I had my young nieces and nephews off at camp with me," Miss Bonner said. "I would run from a spider as though it were a lion. In camp we had a lot of queer animals crawling around the place, particularly huge spiders. I suppose there were not more of them than of other insects, but I was more impressed by the number of them. I discovered that my fear of them had an effect on the children, not only on the girls, but on the small boys in the camp. So I decided to pretend that I was not frightened and would appear quite calm when I was really horribly upset on the inside. I was grateful later on that I did this, because I discovered that by the time we left camp I had lost a goodly part of my fear of spiders as well as teaching the children not to be afraid of them."

"Those are good examples of how fears are built up and also how they are broken down," Mr. Newman said. "It is natural for a child to be more or less afraid of thunder, because at birth he has a fear of sudden loud noises. But whether this fear grows and is carried over to other things or becomes less and less as the years go by depends on what happens to the child. We adults do not realize how children are apt to copy us without thinking about it. Fear is even more contagious than measles and scarlet fever. You know also that even nervousness in a mother has its effect on a child. That is why, when you are very busy or cross or hurried, the children seem to be worse than ever. The baby will cry without any seeming reason, and the older children will fret and fuss. Your being flustered has its effect on your own body, too. But I am thinking now especially of the children in the home and the pupils in our Sunday school classes and how they are affected by what the parent or teacher thinks or feels or does. For what we feel or think usually shows itself in what we do. Have you ever had something happen to you that would show what I mean, Mr. Gordon?" Mr. Newman asked.

"I remember quite well a teacher in Sunday school who seemed to do everything from a sense of duty, even to going on our school picnic each year," Mr. Gordon said. "To this man religion and Church work seemed to be things that bothered him, but that must not be neglected. I shall never forget, either, another teacher who was filled with the joy of Christianity and of doing what he could for others. My class had been poor in attendance under the first man, but we all came whenever possible after this other man began teaching us. We boys felt differently about the work that the class did, and we even carried over the spirit of helpfulness and thoughtfulness into our games together. So I agree with you that the attitude and manner of the teacher is one of the most important things in Church work."

"You see, the way you feel about a thing determines what you are going to do about it," Mr. Newman remarked. "After all, what we do is not the result of *knowing* a thing, but the result of feeling a certain way about it. Mrs. Graham, for instance, said that she knows that she should teach a class, but she 'does not feel like doing it.' Not until she learns to feel differently will she decide to take up such work. It is the same way with our young people and Church work. They may be told again and again that it is their duty to do this or that, but telling them about their duty is not enough to lead them to do it. Sometimes it even 'sets them against it,' because they do not want to be forced to act in certain ways. This independence comes from their desire to feel important and to manage their own affairs, as we said in our second meeting."

"These young people must have plenty of 'feeling' about running around and having a good time," Mr. Brown said. "They surely do enough of that. But I suppose that we are not always wise in simply talking to them about their duty instead of trying to help them learn to do these things of their own accord. As I see it, they will do only those things that bring them some kind of satisfaction. And I agree with you that we may have even turned some of them away from Church work because we have nagged them about it so constantly without trying to follow their interests or longings that we talked about some weeks ago."

"That is quite true," Mr. Newman said. "We should try to guide their interests in certain ways and should remember that we cannot begin too early. The sooner good habits are formed, the better. Also the training and developing of the feelings begins with the babies. You know how easy it is to spoil a baby. He learns to get what he wants by crying for it, and later on he will have a fit of temper and scream and kick in order to make people meet his every wish. Self-control is not something that can be given a child or even something that he can learn in a certain length of time after he reaches the teens. The foundation of it is laid in infancy. A child of three who cries loudly whenever he bumps his head or scratches his finger is getting a start in the wrong direction. His parents should not pet him or 'make over him' whenever he has a slight accident, for that leads him to make a bid for sympathy and attention at the least bit of trouble, instead of learning to bear the pain or discomfort without bothering other people about it. This is a very important question, and I hope you mothers will study the problem again later on."

"My brother-in-law was spoiled when he was a child, and he has little control over his temper," Miss Lane said. "You spoke of an emotion or strong feeling as a 'stirred-up feeling inside.' I think that it changes a person on the outside, too. This brother-in-law looks like a different person when he has one of his attacks of anger. We often fear that he will bring on a stroke of apoplexy. He gets red in the face, shouts, clenches his fists, and looks as though he is ready to knock down anyone who may happen to be near him."

"He not only looks different, but he *is* different," Mr. Newman explained. "Studies have been made of animals and people under violent feelings, and it has been discovered that real changes are taking place in their bodies. Certain fluids that are stored up in their bodies are loosed and go into the blood and change it. Also these liquids make the muscles stronger. You probably remember some wrestling match with a boy, Mr. Brown, when you found this to be true."

"I surely do," Mr. Brown replied. "I was tussling with a boy at school one day, and he tried to throw me unfairly. I was so angry that I felt as though I could whip a giant. And I threw him, too, though he was much bigger than I was. I remember another time when I was very much frightened, and I ran faster than I ever did before or since. I never could understand how that could be so until you said what you did just now."

"Some people have actually died from the effect of very strong feeling or emotion," Mr. Newman added. "And even when feelings are not so violent they are enough to make us less able to do what we want to do. For instance, when we are 'all keyed up' to do a thing and have to wait, it is hard on us. You have had that happen to you if you have run a race. While you were waiting for the signal to start you seemed to lose some of your 'pep' if you had to wait too long. In football or baseball, if the members of one team become very angry they are likely to lose the game. So you see emotions can cause us a lot of trouble. Of course this world would be a dreary place if all of us had no emotions. It is the love of our family and friends, the joy of doing things and of looking at beautiful things, the sympathy that others give us when we are in trouble that make life richer and fuller. We do not want to be upset by too strong emotions, but we want to have quiet and deep feelings that lead us to do the things that make the world a better place in which to live. The love of our Church and of children and the desire to help bring in the kingdom of God will move us to work long and patiently. It will lead us to forget our ease and comfort and do things that call for hard work. Those of us who are willing to give up our evenings to this study and discussion in our Sunday School Council here are making a real sacrifice because the love of God is in us. In olden days it used to be said that the heart was the place where the emotions lay. A beautiful way of expressing what I have been trying to say is as follows: 'Out of the heart are the issues of life.' (Proverbs 4: 23.) That is the reason

132

why it is necessary that we help our pupils have the right feeling about things."

"I see more clearly now what you had in mind when you were talking to us about attitudes and appreciations," Miss Lane said. "Since our discussion about them, I have been trying to find out what my juniors have been learning besides the memory verses and the answers to the questions about the lesson. I see that more important than memorizing passages from the Bible or answering questions are the feelings that pupils have about the Sunday school and the church building and the services and religion and all the rest. But we need some help in leading our pupils to build up the right kind of attitudes. What would you suggest?"

"Can you say, 'Now to-day I am going to have my pupils learn to love nature and the beautiful things in God's world. I will tell them they ought to love them, and I will warn them that if they don't learn to do so to-day we will have to study about the beauty of nature again next Sunday'?" Mr. Newman asked.

"Why, that would be absurd! But I think I see what you are driving at," Miss Lane replied. "We should 'keep children in the presence of beautiful things,' as a wise friend once advised me. We must help them to see the beauty of the flowers and the trees and to be thankful to

God for his wonderful world. Then finally a love and appreciation of these things may come without our saying to them, 'Now you must learn to love Nature.' I believe the same thing is true in learning to love a person. It would be useless to say, 'Now I am going to learn to love so and so.' That would never make you love him. But if this person is kind and gentle and thoughtful toward you and shows that he is interested in you and does things for you, you will very probably learn to love him."

"When we were talking about how we learn," Miss Bonner said, "we spoke of the fact that we learn more than one thing at a time. I see more clearly now that among these other things we learn are the attitudes, or ways we have of feeling and acting. I have been thinking about this, and I remember one thing a teacher told me once about learning. He said that the important thing was *learning to live*. Of course it is important to learn certain facts, but what we do with these facts is more important still, and we have just been saying that what we do will depend on how we feel. I believe this is something we ought to think about carefully, not only now, but in all the work that we will do with Sunday school pupils. To me it seems that this carries us back to the chief aim of our Sunday school work—to help people *learn to live* as Jesus would have them live."

134

CHAPTER IX

THEY NEED HELP IN MANY WAYS

"DURING the time between our meetings here each week," Mr. Morris said, "some of us parents and teachers have talked at odd moments about certain problems which we have not discussed here. We realize now more fully that children need help in building up the right kinds of interests, in learning, in forming attitudes and habits, and in controlling their feelings. There are a number of other points on which we need guidance ourselves in order that we may know how to guide our children, and I suggest that we take these up this evening. For example, I have been thinking a lot of what you said about why children are constantly active. I had never understood before why they are on the go all the time, though since I have five of them I know that it is not in their nature to be still. What I am puzzled about is why they are always pulling things to pieces or breaking them up and why they find so much pleasure in doing it. They are much more apt to destroy things than they are to make them."

"You feel that way mainly because you are more interested in the things they tear up or break than in the things they make," Mrs. Gordon said. "For instance, suppose your boy and his gang are making a shed to use

135

as a meeting place. If he breaks your hammer that you lent to him you are very much upset, and you tell him that he is not careful and that he ruins half of the things that he touches. But you pay no attention to the fact that he and his little friends have really been very clever in building a shed that will actually hold together even when the wind blows. I speak from experience with my own children, for my aunt pointed this out to me recently. She told me that I had talked for years about how Sue had once pulled off the arms and legs of one of her dolls, but that I had not seemed to notice now how smart she was in 'rigging up' little hats for her dolls out of scraps of ribbon and silk and in making some furniture for her dolls' house. This made me watch for the things that my children made. I was surprised to find out how clever they were in making good use of materials that I should have considered worthless."

"Perhaps they are simply curious and often tear up a toy 'to see how it is put together,' " Mrs. Ray suggested. "That is what my little boy said to me the other day when I asked him why he had taken the wheels off his new toy cart. After I had told a neighbor about this, she said that her little girl had stuck a knife in her doll 'to see what made her so hard.' "

"I am sure that curiosity is one of the chief reasons why they destroy things, as you suggest," Mr. Newman

136

said. "We adults have lived long enough to learn a good deal about various things, and we take them for granted. But the world is all so new to little folks that they are continually poking and pulling and trying to turn things inside out. One reason for this is that they are interested in making things happen, as we learned in one of our early discussions. Even though a child loves to play with a balloon he may not be able to resist the temptation to stick a pin in it to see it collapse or to hear the funny noise that it makes when it bursts. Making a noise, by the way, is great sport for most small boys and a good many big ones. That is an easy and simple way of 'doing something'; and the louder they can shout or beat a drum, the better pleased they are. Some men show this desire when they turn on the radio so that it deafens one. And have you ever seen a father blow his boy's horn or bugle until the son has to beg for a chance to do it?"

The members of the group smiled, and a number of the men looked rather sheepish.

"Don't you think it is a good plan to let children experiment with at least some of their toys?" Miss Bonner asked. "I think this is a good way for them to find out about how things work, and they never will learn much except through experience. Of course I do not believe in letting them destroy everything they have, but it is a

137

good plan to give them toys with which they can tinker, pulling them apart and putting them together. Sometimes when a child has ruined one of his playthings he will beg to have it 'fixed up' again. They are not always able to see beforehand what is going to happen, and they are much surprised at what they have done."

"Another way they have of learning about things is by asking questions," Miss Hopkins said. "Things that are commonplace to us will arouse their curiosity, and you parents and teachers know how many questions they can ask in one day's time."

"I should say we do," Mrs. Chapman sighed. "And such queer ideas they often have, too! A few days ago, when my family was riding far out in the country to see my father, my six-year-old Margaret, who had been quiet for some time, said thoughtfully: 'When it gets dark, it is darker in the country than it is in town.' So I tried to explain to her that the streets of a town were usually brighter than a country lane because there were more lights in town. When children make queer statements I do not believe it is right to say, 'Why, that is a foolish notion! How did you ever think of that? I remember when I was little my mother took care to answer my questions as best she could instead of telling me to run along and play and not bother her. She seemed to have real

138

respect for me and my questions, and she felt that I was due her attention and interest just as an adult was."

"Because you answer her questions, Mrs. Chapman, I see a difference between Margaret and the other members of her class," Mrs. Sanders said. "Every little while I am surprised at how much she knows about things that the other children are ignorant about. You should be pleased to know that you help her so much."

"I know a little boy who bothers his mother with the most foolish questions imaginable," Mrs. Ray said. "He seems to enjoy trying to puzzle her, though I confess that she always tries to hush him up and doesn't bother to teach him anything by talking with him. What do you think makes him do that way?"

"One thing that you said shows what the trouble probably is," Mr. Newman answered. "She 'tries to hush him up' and rarely pays much attention to him. Now remember that we all crave attention and long to feel important. The boy's desire for this may not be satisfied, and he may have formed the habit of getting attention by asking questions. Some of them may show that he really wants to learn something, but others may be merely a way of making his mother know that he is around and he prefers being told to 'run along' to being ignored altogether."

"You have explained the reason for something I wanted to ask you about this evening," Mr. Morris said. "I heard a story recently of a child who acted very rudely when her mother had company. When, later on, she was scolded for it, she exclaimed: 'Well, you wouldn't pay any attention to me so long as I was good when the company was here, so I just had to do something.' I did not realize that this was another case of a child trying to win attention. However, I believe that we should be very careful about deciding whether or not our children are in earnest about asking questions."

"That is very true, Mr. Morris," Mr. Newman said. "People can learn a great deal through questioning, and we should help children get information in this way. As we said earlier in the evening, many things that seem quite commonplace to us are new and fascinating to children, and we do not want to crush out their curiosity and imagination. They need these traits. It is a pity that frequently adults have lost them because when they were growing up they were not encouraged to wonder about things and to try to figure things out. Our scientists and inventors and explorers are blessed with much curiosity and imagination. Before Lindbergh flew to France he probably dreamed about blazing a path across the skies, and I am sure that he could not have worked out plans for the trip if he had not had both curiosity and imagination."

"I never thought of it in that way before," Mrs. Sanders

said, "but I surely do not need to encourage my little Rachel to use her imagination now. She tells the most fanciful stories. She seems to live in another world with fairies and Brownies and tame tigers and butterflies that talk. Sometimes, too, she will insist for a day or so that she is not herself, but is another little girl. She then insists that I call her Arabella, and she has a wonderful time 'pretending things.' "

"That is natural with many children," Miss Bonner remarked. "My young nephew, George, used to have an imaginary playmate. For a whole year George played games with 'Jimmy' and would run races with him or read aloud to him for hours at a time. This was a fortunate thing, because there were no children living near George's home in the country, and being able to pretend as he did kept him from being lonesome. He finally became tired of his invisible playmate, however. One rainy day, when he was restless because he had a cold and could not go out of doors, his mother asked him why he did not play with Jimmy. 'O, he has gone to Chicago to see his grandmother!' George said. And that was the last of Jimmy."

"Pretending is all right if it is not carried too far," said Mr. Chester, "but I have known children to lie about

141

things, saying that they saw bears in the yard or a dog as big as a horse."

"My Rachel has been telling me tales like that recently," Mrs. Gordon said, "but I do not think that she is lying in the sense that grown folks lie. She is not telling an untruth in order to get out of an embarrassing situation or to avoid blame or punishment. I am trying to teach her that she must let me know when she is pretending and when she actually means what she says, though of course I usually know without her telling me. She is learning that I will enter into her games of pretending, but that I expect her to know the difference between saying that the fairies came to her tea party and saying that she had not touched a cup that she took off the pantry shelf and broke. When her father tells her a story at bedtime he asks whether she wants a 'make-believe one or a really true one,' and after she makes her choice he tells her either a fairy tale or a story of something that he and his sister did when they were about her age."

"I believe, as you do, that it would be dangerous if she should continue to tell 'big tales' when she is older, but I think there is no harm for her to do it at her age," Mr. Newman said. "Grown people are inclined to take things literally and expect each other to be accurate in what they say. Children have not learned to do that, because of their vivid imaginations and their lack of experience.

For instance, they do not measure things as adults do. John's grandfather, who has a farm in the next county, lives 'a thousand or three thousand miles from here.' Last Sunday I heard two small boys talking about what time it was. One of them said that it was twenty minutes to eleven. The other said, 'I wish it was a hundred minutes to eleven.' Not to be outdone, the first one went even further: 'I wouldn't care if it was a million minutes to eleven.' "

"Yes," Miss Hopkins agreed, "they certainly exaggerate and 'talk big' without meaning anything by it. A little boy who insists that he could eat twenty-five saucers of ice cream would be put to it to eat the fourth saucer. We laugh at things like this and at the tales they tell us of fairies and of the hundreds of cats behind the barn, but when they use their imagination about things with which we are concerned ourselves, such as why they took so long to come home from a neighbor's house, we scold them or even punish them."

"What I want to know is, why they can't reason things out any better," Mr. Chester remarked. "Some of their ideas are surely queer."

"A child three years of age may reason, and he does it just as adults do," Mr. Newman said. "However, his world is so small and he has had experience with such

143

a limited number of things that he often reaches a wrong conclusion. Little Margaret had really reasoned when she told her mother that it was darker in the country than it was in town, but she had not taken all the facts into account. Another example is that of a five-year-old child in a certain city who likes to cook biscuits for her dolls when the negro cook makes the biscuits for the family. One day, as the child was kneading the piece of dough that the cook had given her, she looked at the piece she had and then at the white batch that the colored woman was handling. 'Aunt Ann,' she asked, 'what makes black folks' dough white and white folks' dough black?' Clearly that was reasoning, but she had failed to notice her own dirty little hands."

"I agree with you that children can reason," Mr. Gordon said, "but don't you believe that most of what we do is done from habit rather than from thinking things through?"

"Yes, I do," Mr. Newman said. "That is why it is exceedingly important that we help children form the right kind of habits. A noted teacher once stated that not even adults think until they run up against problems that stump them and make them stop to think."

"A question that I have been wanting to ask you for some time, Mr. Newman, is, How can we lead our pupils to have strong wills?" Mrs. Sanders said. "Some of the children in my Sunday school class try to get their own way, but that is pure stubbornness. What I am interested in is that they have will power."

"That is a good point you made about the difference between will and stubbornness," Mr. Newman said. "But, first of all, I want to ask you what you mean when you speak of *will*."

"Why, I never tried to explain what it is," Mrs. Sanders remarked; "but, at any rate, it is what makes you go ahead when you have a hard job and would like to give up. A person with a weak will couldn't be depended on to keep at the job."

"I used to think that one's will was something that could be developed like one's muscles and was a part of one's character set aside to overlook what one did," Miss Bonner added. "I believe quite differently now, however. It seems to me that we say that a person has a strong will when we feel that we can depend on him to act in certain ways, as Mrs. Sanders suggested. Now, one person may always act in ways that are honest and fair, and another person will act in opposite ways. Yet both of them would be said to have strong wills, provided they carried out their ideas without being turned aside. From our discussion of habit, I discovered that we act in one way or another mainly because we have learned to act in that way.

145

Do you think that you can help build up a child's will by helping him form certain habits of acting?"

"I do, Miss Bonner, and I believe that you have the key to the facts in that statement of yours," Mr. Newman answered. "Will power is not a mysterious thing that we have when we are born, but is built up by making right choices again and again until habits of such choices become part of our nature. To me this is a very encouraging idea, for it gives us hope that we may be able to help our pupils *develop* strong wills. For example, if John has habits of making wrong choices, we may help him form habits of making right choices. Now, that is a very difficult task, but we may count ourselves coworkers with God when we try to lead our children to build strong characters in this way."

"As we have talked together here I have come to realize something that I had thought of vaguely before," Mrs. Gordon put in. "That is, we cannot separate a child into divisions and think of his body and spirit and mind as things that have little connection with each other, but we must think of him as a 'whole' child. For example, some one said once that '*all* of Johnny comes to the breakfast table each morning and stays together all during the day.' I have heard that fact spoken of as 'the unity, or oneness, of life,' and I think that is a good way to put it. An outsider who heard our discussions might wonder why we Sunday school teachers have been talking about play and reading and why a child is active; but all such things are a part of his life, and we must work with the *whole* child."

"I am glad you brought that out, Mrs. Gordon," Mr. Newman said. "You are right in saying that we should not think of some things as being religious and others as not being religious. Everything that we do and feel and say and think is part of our character and should be tested in the light of what Jesus would say about it. And when we help a child make right use of his imagination and curiosity, or to reason things out correctly, or to take proper care of his body, or to form good habits of any kind, we are helping him to grow in character. Nothing in the life of a child is so small or insignificant that it does not deserve the attention of those who are leading him to live as Jesus would have him live. Next week we shall have our last meeting, and I hope that we can then talk more fully about growth in religion. This idea has run like a thread throughout our discussions, but I feel that it will be well for us to give a whole evening to it."

CHAPTER X

HOW DO THEY GROW IN RELIGION?

"There is one thing that I have been thinking about a lot recently as I have been working with my class of beginners," Mrs. Sanders said. "I should like for all of you to help me answer this question: 'Can a little child be a Christian?'"

"I believe your answer to that question will depend on what you mean when you say that a person is a Christian," Miss Bonner said. "If you said that an adult was a Christian, you would probably mean that he believed and thought and acted in certain ways and that he could be depended on to do the right things—the things that Jesus would have him do. We cannot expect a child to accept Jesus and to follow him in just the way that a grown person would, but he can be a *child* Christian in his own small world."

Mrs. Gordon then spoke up: "I always think of a little tot as being in the kingdom and being one of God's children because of what Jesus said. When he was explaining to his disciples what they should be like in order to be true followers of his, he did not point to any well-known godly men and say, 'Be like these fine men, and you will please me.' Instead he took a little child and set him in the midst and said, 'Unless you become as little children you cannot enter the kingdom.' I believe that by this he meant that we should have a childlike faith in God and express our faith in simplicity and trust and wonder, in order to be followers of Jesus."

"Some of the Church fathers spoke again and again of children as being 'born into this world in Christ the Redeemer,' " Mr. Morris said. "As Miss Bonner points out, we cannot expect so much of children as we can of young people or of adults. I have studied this problem a great deal, and I have watched children as they have become more and more able to live as Jesus would have them live. I believe it would help us in our thinking if we tried to figure out what we mean when we say that a person is learning to follow Jesus. And the first question I should like to ask is, whether or not we can say a person is growing in religion if he does right only because he is *made* to do so."

"No, I believe you have to *want* to do right without being forced, in order to please Jesus," Miss Bonner said. "We must learn to choose the right thing of our own accord when we are faced with the temptation to do the wrong thing. For example, you could not say that a man was honest if he stole when he had a chance to do so and was careful not to steal only when he knew that he was being watched."

"Do you think that a child two years old who takes a toy that belongs to another child is stealing?" Mrs. Sanders asked. "That is a problem that I have been facing with my own little boy, but I cannot feel that he is really a thief."

"Of course he is not stealing," Mrs. Gordon hastened to say. "Most of us mothers have had to face such problems, but I do not believe that little children are wicked when they do things like that. A little child does not realize the difference between what belongs to him and what belongs to other people, and until he learns this difference he is not stealing and is therefore not sinning. It is the job of his parents and his teachers to help him learn to respect the rights and belongings of others. A baby will grab for anything he sees, with no thought of *mine* or *yours*. He claims everything as his own—my ball, my mamma, my car, my puppy—and probably plays with whatever he can get his hands on until the other children in the family have to hide their treasures to keep them from him. He learns gradually that some things belong to him and other things belong to mother and father and brother. To help him learn this lesson I believe that we should give a child some things of his own and make him responsible for taking care of them. Even a child of two or three can put up his toys and can feed his kitten or dog, for example."

"That is a good plan, Mrs. Gordon," Mr. Newman said. "We do need to help our children learn the difference between what belongs to them and what belongs to other people. Also we need to teach them the difference between the right and the wrong in other things. For example, some weeks ago a little friend of mine who is seven years old told me that she was studying 'adding' in school and remarked quite frankly that one day when she did not know how to add two numbers she looked on the paper of the girl next to her and copied the answer. She did not feel that there was anything wrong about this act. It was the first time that she had found herself in a difficulty of that sort, and she took the easiest way out of it without stopping to think whether or not she should do it. If she had cheated deliberately as an older child might have done, there would have been a different kind of problem for me to face in trying to lead her to see that she was 'taking something that did not belong to her.' Often we make the mistake of scolding children and talking to them about things that they do not understand. We tell them that they must be polite or honest or generous without helping them see what these words mean. It reminds me of the little girl whose mother used to punish her severely for 'not telling the truth.' One day when she was being spanked the child wailed: 'Well, I'd tell the truth if you would tell me what the *truth* is!' We

151

must help a child see that to 'be polite' is to open the door for grandmother, to wait for others to stop speaking instead of breaking in on a conversation, to say 'Good morning' to the grocery boy, and so forth. Only after he has had many such experiences as this will a child learn what it means to 'be polite.' He builds up his ideas of what politeness is from many examples of it and from having his parents praise him for being polite in these definite ways. Jesus taught us in this way the great lesson of love. He did not say, 'You must live a life of love and thoughtfulness,' and then let us guess at what he meant. He gave us enough examples of what such love is for us to understand what he meant. He told us the story of the Good Samaritan. He said for us to love our enemies as well as our friends, to do good to those who were not good to us, to care so much for the poor that we are willing to give up riches to help those who are not so fortunate as we are. Then when he had made his idea clear to us he said that we must follow that same law of love in everything we do. With a little child one has to have more patience and give more examples than with a grown person, for the child cannot understand the meaning of words that adults have learned. It is a difficult thing to teach children as I have suggested, but it is the only fair thing to do, and they will learn faster if they are guided by older people."

152

"I agree with you, Mr. Newman," Mr. Morris said. "If we do not help them learn the difference between right and wrong ways of doing things, we expect too much of them. We forget that they do not know the things that we know, and instead of being patient with them we are likely to fuss at them because they have not chosen the right thing. And there is another point that I am particularly interested in—that is, we must help them learn to choose for themselves without depending on their parents to do the choosing for them. Unless we do this, when they are young folks they will not have had any practice in thinking things through before they make their choices and will often choose too hastily. I know that some of you are thinking that the young people of to-day rarely ask for advice from their elders, but are inclined to decide rashly to do something and then go ahead and do it without stopping to think of what may come of it. But I believe that if we helped them build up habits of thinking things through and looking at both sides of a question before acting we should not have so much trouble with them as we are having to-day. When they were children we usually decided everything for them and then expected them to learn suddenly to make their own decisions. When we help them choose in a great many little ways we are really helping them develop the power to make their choices in big things later on."

153

"My sister with whom I live is having difficulty with her son and her daughter along this very line," Miss Hopkins said. "She did not realize until recently that she had always made decisions for her children instead of helping them think things through for themselves. For example, she chose the material for Helen's dresses and selected the patterns and the trimmings even after her daughter was a young lady. Helen married three years ago and now has a baby, but she never knows what kind of cloth to buy or how to make a dress for herself or her baby after she has bought the material. My sister was scolding her about it the other day when she came over to our house to get some help. Helen flared up and said: 'Well, you never did let me choose my clothes before I married, so it is your own fault that I don't know anything about it. It is the same way with cooking, too. You always said that you could do it more easily than you could tell me, and I have had a hard time learning how to cook. And you are rearing Jim just the same way. Whenever he earns any money, either in the store or by helping on the farm, you and dad tell him just what you think he ought to do with it. Yet if Jim marries in the next few years he will have to earn money for his family and decide how to spend it, though he has no idea now of the value of a dollar.' My sister has been much worried about it, because she realizes that what Helen said is true."

"That is a good illustration of what we have been discussing," Mr. Newman said. "Of course our decisions vary with our age, and we choose between different types of things when we are four or fourteen or forty. A little child, for example, does not choose between being honest and dishonest in the same way that an adolescent would. The child is learning to choose whether he will cry and fret, or smile, and whether or not he will share his toys with a little playmate. A boy fourteen years of age chooses between such things as cheating on examination and being fair, playing marbles for keeps and not doing so, and sulking or being a good sport in a game of tennis. A business man chooses between joining others in a crooked deal or refusing to do so, between being honest or dishonest when he sells groceries or cattle. In all of our choices we are growing and changing, and we hope that each year we will reach higher levels of Christian living."

"This discussion has made me think of something that has puzzled me a good deal," Mrs. Chapman said. "The majority of the children in my class never have any money of their own, and when they are ready to start to Sunday school their parents give them the nickels or pennies that they bring for the offering. When this is done, it is hard

155

to teach the children to be willing to make a sacrifice in order to help other people. They have no chance to make a choice as to what to do with money that is actually their own."

"I believe the best plan is for the parents to let each child in the family have a certain amount of money each week for his very own, even though it may be only ten cents," Mr. Gordon suggested. "Then the child can decide for himself what to do with his money. With this arrangement, any offering that the child makes will represent his own choice and his interest in carrying on the work of his class in missions or social service or in other lines."

"That plan of an allowance may work sometimes, but there are dangers in it," Miss Lane pointed out. "Sometimes a child may use all his money for candy or marbles or something else that he wants. Occasionally some of the boys and girls in my class keep the money that their parents give them for the offering and spend it in one of the ways that I mentioned. Don't you think that is wrong?"

"Yes, it is," Mr. Newman agreed. "But has a child learned to be unselfish in giving when his father sees to it that he puts in the basket for the offering a penny that was given to him for that purpose? He may put the penny in the basket, but at the same time he may be longing to keep the penny, and wishing that he could pretend to put it in without doing so. This builds up the wrong kind of attitude. Now let us see why a child may keep for his own use the money given to him for Sunday school. You remember that at our first meetings we talked about what all of us want—the things that we are interested in. People of different ages have different interests, but we adults sometimes forget that and expect children to have the same desires and wants that we have. A little boy is not often tremendously interested in buying Sunday school literature or in mission work. However, he is much concerned about certain toys or other things to play with. Also his longing for food, especially something sweet, is very strong, and this longing is much more intense than his interest in people in China or India. When he buys candy he satisfies his hunger. When he gives money 'to the Sunday school' what pleasure does he get out of it? He does like to do what the others do, but we decided that when we have two or more interests at the same time the one that is the strongest is the one that leads us to act. What we should like to do as teachers is to lead our pupils to want to give their money to Sunday school work. Can we *make* them want to do this?"

"I don't think so," Miss Bonner said. "As we found out previously, when we try to make them do things the pupils may really be turned against doing them. Our pupils are continually building up habits of feeling about things—their attitudes—which will lead them to act in certain ways. Now that I think about it, I see that feelings or emotions are in reality practically the same as attitudes."

"The problem here is, how can we lead the pupils to become so interested in the Sunday school that they will want to work in it and give money to it?" Mr. Newman suggested. "We want our boys and girls to make the right kind of choices in what they do with their time and money. But this matter of choice is not limited to such things as these. For instance, how many of you have been troubled by the lack of order in your classes?"

Two or three of the teachers spoke at the same time. "You remember that my boys used to throw paper wads in class," Miss Hopkins said, "and no amount of scolding seemed to help; but I have found some ways of appealing to their interests, and when I can do that they pay attention."

"As you discovered, it is difficult to change them by merely scolding them or talking to them," Mr. Newman said. "As we said last week, they will change their ways of behaving only when their feelings have been changed. We want to help them to feel so much interest in the work that they will *choose* to pay attention. This will mean that they have not been forced to do the right thing, but

158

have decided to do it themselves. Now, it is much more difficult to lead them to do this than it is to fuss at them or to order them to keep quiet. The same thing is true in the home. It is easier to do a thing yourself than it is to try to teach the boys and girls to do it. Also it is easier to scold them about not doing what is right than it is to lead them to do the right. Unless somebody helps them to learn to take over responsibilities themselves, however, they will not develop. And to learn a thing means that one must have practice in actually doing it, as we have found out. [See Chapters IV and V.] We try to lead them to keep order in class and to give money because they want to. In this way they will have practice in wanting to do these things."

"Since we have been discussing during the past weeks the problems of the way people feel about things and the danger of forcing children or young folks to do things," Mr. Gordon said, "I have been watching closely quite a number of persons and find that what we have said here in our talks is certainly true. A harsh command to do a certain thing may cause a boy or girl of almost any age to be set against it. Before I thought about this question I would have said that the way children and young people disobey their parents and teachers is a sign of pure contrariness or of a wicked nature, but I see now that we adults have a good deal to do with how boys and girls act.

159

It may often make a bad situation worse if too strict orders are given. For instance, suppose that a boy and a girl read trashy books or go to poor picture shows. If their parents demand that they give up these things, they may do them on the sly. And if that happens, they are not only doing something that we know is bad for them, but they are learning also to deceive their parents. All this reminds me of our discussion about the fact that people learn more than one thing at a time."

"I agree with you that our children should be obedient," Mr. Morris said, "but there are different kinds of obedience. One child may obey his parents willingly and cheerfully because he and his father and mother are good pals and often talk over what he does and why he should do certain things, and he has confidence in their judgment about things that he does not see the reason for. Another boy may obey his parents, but be resentful because he is forced to carry out their orders without a chance to say anything about how he feels and what he wants. He thinks that his parents are not fair to him, and he sulks or has a violent fit of anger. One of the great dangers in punishing children is that they may feel that they have not been treated squarely. Think about your own childhood and talk with other adults about this, and you will be surprised to find out how many grown folks still resent certain punishments that their parents gave them when they were quite young. Some parents punish unjustly because they do not know all the facts. In any case, such an experience is very unfortunate because it builds up in a child the wrong kind of attitude."

"May we take up another point that I have been thinking about?" Miss Bonner asked. "I know that when I have led one of my pupils to do the right thing just one time, it is not enough. I want to be able to rely on him to do the right thing every time. Perhaps that has something to do with being a Christian. We spoke awhile ago about a person who was honest only when he knew that he was being watched. He certainly knew the difference between being honest and being dishonest, but he chose the right only when he saw that it was wise to do so. He did the choosing himself, too, yet he was not really honest, because he would steal if he had a good chance to do so without being caught. I think that we cannot call a person a Christian until we can depend on him. And I suppose that means that he has the habit of doing right, since habits are so much a part of life."

"Yes," Mr. Newman said, "and for that reason we must be careful to see that our pupils have some sort of satisfaction from making right choices about a great many things. It is only in this way that they will build up habits of so many kinds that they can be depended on to do

161

right in all sorts of situations. Of course the habits that they form will vary according to age, as we pointed out before."

"I believe one of the chief things that Jesus expects of us is that we think about other people," Mrs. Ray said. "So how can a little child be a Christian when he is interested mainly in himself?"

"It seems to me that it is a matter of growth and development in this as well as in everything else that we have been talking about during this hour," Mrs. Sanders said. "We easily see that children change as far as their bodies are concerned. The tiny baby becomes a sturdy boy, and then an awkward young man, and finally grows to be as tall as his father. And I think that children develop gradually in other ways. Earlier in the evening we were talking about how a baby learns slowly the difference between what belongs to him and what belongs to other people. And in the same fashion he learns slowly to think of other people in an unselfish way. We should try to lead him to do this more and more until he forms the habit of being always thoughtful and considerate of others instead of putting himself first. How unselfish a person is when he is an adult depends to a large extent on how well he has formed a habit of being so in childhood and adolescence."

"I want to ask for a list of the points that we have

162

talked about this evening, like the lists that we have some-times made before," Miss Lane said. The members of the group agreed to this, and the following points were made:

1. The person himself must know the difference between right and wrong ways of acting.

2. The person himself must choose the right way of acting. He must do it of his own free will instead of being forced to do it.

3. Choosing the right way of acting *once* is not enough. He must form habits of doing the right thing so that he can be depended upon at all times and in all places.

4. When he makes his choice, he must think of other people rather than only of what he wants himself.

"That is a good list of things that we should keep in mind," Mr. Morris said. "To put it another way, we might say that in order to be moral the individual must know and must choose for himself ways of acting for the good of the group, these ways of acting being so often repeated that they become habits. However, I think that we might possibly carry out these points in training a child and still not lead him to be a Christian. In other words, I believe that we have not yet spoken definitely enough about the fact of God in the life of the child. As one writer has put it, we must depend on 'the grace of God to reach out and touch the life of the child.' Beginning

163

early in life, there should be a growing sense of the presence of God and a finer and deeper realization of one's relation to him. It is this discovery of God by the person and the part that God has in leading the person to this discovery that makes our religious education different from other kinds of education."

"I am glad you brought out that point if I had not made it clear myself," Mr. Newman said. "Perhaps I was taking too much for granted in our discussions here. These ideas that you have just expressed so well have been in my mind all along when I have spoken of our living together as Jesus would have us live. In Jesus we have the great example of a perfect relationship with God, and we want to lead our children to feel that God is ever near and that he will help them as they make their choices. In fact, the presence of God should become so much a part of us that it floods our lives just as the sunlight floods the air on a bright summer day. This is what I meant when I said in our meeting last week that to a Christian everything in life is religious. We cannot think of any part of our life as separate from all the rest of it. As we mentioned before, that is why we have spent so much time talking about the longings and desires that people have, about play and imagination and how people learn, and what effect their surroundings have on them. We cannot think of religion as set apart from our work and play and business and family relations and attitudes toward other races and all the rest of our lives. In all of these things we are coworkers with God in leading our pupils to choose the Christian way of life even when they are tempted to choose a way that is unchristian."

"I was sure you agreed with me," Mr. Morris said. "We believe that both children and adults can grow in religion, and it is our privilege to lead them to understand more and more clearly what it means to be a child of God."

"There is one thing further that I want to say," Miss Bonner remarked. "At times I have wondered why we have spent more time in talking about children than about young people or adults. But though at first I could not see the reason for this emphasis on childhood, I see more clearly now that in order to understand young people and adults you must know how their interests have changed and developed and what training they had when they were young. Even though you cannot know exactly what happened to each person while growing up, you may be able to get a fairly clear idea of how children develop and to see the importance of training."

"You are right, Miss Bonner," Mr. Newman said. "The foundation of all later life is laid in the early years. While grown folks can overcome to a large extent some harmful influences of childhood, they will never be what they would have been if they had not been under these influences. We cannot begin too early in teaching children to form good habits and attitudes. And in all our efforts we should realize that we are the channels through which God is made real to other people and that on our shoulders as parents and teachers lies the difficult but highest task of helping children, young people, and adults to live more and more as Jesus would have them live, which means growth in religion."

APPENDIX

I. Notes and References

There has been no opportunity in the compass of this small textbook to consider many topics of importance to the parent and teacher, but it is hoped that this brief introduction to pupil study will be an incentive to the readers of the book to continue their work until they are able to make a practical application of the chief principles of psychology.

The notes below are to take the place of footnotes throughout the book, and may serve as a guide to the student who desires to do further reading.

Chapter I

Some of the historic aims of religious education are as follows: To teach the Bible, to train people to become efficient members of the Church, to save one's soul, to prepare for the next world.

These aims have changed in recent years in line with developing theories and practice in the field of education. To-day we consider education not as the transmission of knowledge, but with Dewey we think of it as the process of continually reconstructing the experience of the individual with the purpose of promoting the aims and ideals of the group. Soares thinks of religious education as the "process of helping growing persons achieve religious experience"—that is, "the sharing with some worshiping group the experience of that divine purpose of righteousness and love which gives meaning to life viewed as a whole, and a consequent experience of growing competence to meet life as a total situation." Coe says: "Christian education is to be thought of as . . . the Christian religion in operation."

> Coe: "A Social Theory of Religious Education;" "What Is Christian Education?"
> Emme and Stevick: "Principles of Religious Education."
> Hickman: "Can Religion Be Taught?"
> Myers: "What Is Religious Education?"
> Soares: "Principles of Religious Education."
> Vieth: "Objectives in Religious Education."

Chapters II and III

The terms "instinct" and "instinctive tendencies" are not used in this discussion. These drives or urges, which are present at birth, are spoken of as longings or desires or wants. They are given in everyday language in Overstreet's "Influencing Human Behavior," Chapter II, "The Appeal to Wants." McDougall classifies instincts and indicates the emotion that accompanies each. In Volume I of his "Educational Psychology" and in Part I of his "Briefer Course," Thorndike lists what he considers to be the chief instincts. John B. Watson, the leader of the school of Behaviorism, believes only in neural reactions and unfortunately finds no place in his mechanistic philosophy for thinking or consciousness or the finer things of the Spirit.

Norsworthy and Whitley: "Psychology of Childhood."

Overstreet: "Influencing Human Behavior."

Thorndike: "Educational Psychology," Vol. I, "The Original Nature of Man;" "Educational Psychology, Briefer Course," Part I.

McDougall: "Outlines of Psychology;" "Social Psychology."

Woodworth: "Psychology—A Study of Mental Life;" "Dynamic Psychology."

Sheridan: "Growth in Religion."

Chapters IV and V

In these chapters the physiological basis of habit is not explained, though knowledge of this is necessary for one who would adequately understand the foundation of habitual action.

Thorndike has stated the laws of learning as follows: Law of Readiness; Law of Exercise—Use and Disuse; Law of Effect—Satisfaction or Pleasure, Dissatisfaction or Annoyance.

A fine though simple discussion of learning is given in Kilpatrick's "Foundations of Method," and the diagrams that he borrows from various psychologies are helpful.

This book is invaluable to teachers in both Sunday school and day school, for it deals not only with the learning process, but with the formation of attitudes, the effect of coercion, the wider problem of method, moral training, and similar topics.

In this chapter no distinction is made between "readiness" and "mind-set," though the latter is the more inclusive term.

Thorndike: "Educational Psychology," Vol. II, "The Learning Process;" "Educational Psychology, Briefer Course," Part II; "Adult Learning."
Kilpatrick: "Foundations of Method."
Norsworthy and Whitley: "Psychology of Childhood."
Gates: "Psychology for Students of Education."
Mossman: "Teaching and Learning in the Elementary School."
Charters: "The Teaching of Ideals."
Sheridan: "Growth in Religion."

Chapter VI

The direct relation of physical well-being and morals has been realized more fully in recent years. It is one of the responsibilities of the Church to provide for its members recreation that is joyous and that will also promote health. The suggestions in this chapter about arranging and equipping a playground could be followed with little financial outlay, though they would require some time and effort. Also provision should be made to guide the reading interests of the Sunday school pupils. A good library, even though small, may furnish much pleasure on rainy days or when other activities fail to appeal.

> Norsworthy and Whitley: "Psychology of Childhood."
> Lucas: "The Health of the Runabout Child."
> Sheridan: "Growth in Religion."

On sex education:

> Eddy: "Sex and Youth."
> Sanger: "What Every Boy and Girl Should Know."
> Gray: "Men, Women, and God."
> Gruenberg: "Parents and Sex Education."
> Bigelow: "Sex Education."

Chapter VII

The laws of individual differences are given in full in Volume III of Thorndike's "Educational Psychology" and in less detail in his "Briefer Course." Norsworthy and Whitley follow him in their discussion of these laws in "The Psychology of Childhood."

> Thorndike: "Educational Psychology," Vol. III, "Individual Differences;" "Educational Psychology, Briefer Course," Part III.
> Woodworth: "Psychology—A Study of Mental Life."
> Garrison and Garrison: "The Psychology of Elementary School Subjects."

Chapter VIII

Some one has said that the history of the world is the history of the emotional reactions of the human race.

The development and control of the emotions is undoubtedly one of the most vital as well as one of the most puzzling problems that parents and teachers face. The foundation for the control of the feelings is laid in the early years of a child's life, beginning in infancy with such things as learning not to cry. A child who is spoiled has no adequate preparation for proper emotional balance in youth and adulthood.

> Morgan: "The Psychology of the Unadjusted School Child."
> Groves: "Wholesome Childhood."
> Pierce: "Understanding Our Children."
> Overstreet: "About Ourselves."
> Woodworth: "Psychology—A Study of Mental Life."
> Zachry: "Personality Adjustments of School Children."

Chapter IX

In view of the unity of life, there is no factor that does not influence one's religious nature. As Gibran, the Indian poet, says, "What is my religion but my life?"

Many problems, such as fighting, stealing, general disobedience, "talking back," using "bad words," the harmful effect of continual nagging, and the like are not dealt with

172

in this chapter. The references given below will be particularly valuable to those who are troubled with such problems.

Norsworthy and Whitley: "Psychology of Childhood."

Watson: "Case Studies for Teachers of Religion."

Skinner, Gast, and Skinner: "Readings in Educational Psychology."

Gruenberg: "Guidance of Childhood and Youth—Readings in Child Study."

Thom: "Everyday Problems of the Everyday Child."

Chapter X

This is not intended to be a consideration of conversion or of educational evangelism or of theological questions, but is a brief statement of how Sunday school teachers as well as parents may help their pupils to live as Jesus would have them live. For some of the basic ideas in this chapter the author is indebted to the chapter on moral education in "Psychology of Childhood," by Norsworthy and Whitley.

Sheridan: "Growth in Religion."

Norsworthy and Whitley: "Psychology of Childhood."

Kilpatrick: "Foundations of Method."

Hartshorne: "Childhood and Character."

II. For Further Reading

American Social Hygiene Association: Pamphlets on Sex Education.

Bigelow: "Sex Education."

Blanton and Blanton: "Child Guidance."

Charters: "The Teachings of Ideals."

Chave: "The Junior."

Coe: "A Social Theory of Religious Education;" "The Motives of Men;" "What Is Christian Education?" "What Ails Our Youth?"

Dixon: "Children Are Like That."

Eddy: "Sex and Youth."

Emme and Stevick: "Principles of Religious Education."

Gates: "Psychology for Students of Education."

Garrison and Garrison: "The Psychology of Elementary School Subjects."

Gray: "Men, Women, and God."

Groves: "Wholesome Childhood."

Gruenberg: "Guidance of Childhood and Youth."

Hickman: "Can Religion Be Taught?"

Hollingworth, H. L.: "Mental Growth and Decline."

Hollingworth, L. S.: "The Psychology of the Adolescent."

James: "Psychology, Briefer Course."

Kilpatrick: "Foundations of Method."

Lucas: "The Health of the Runabout Child."

Mateer: "Just Normal Children."

McDougall: "Outline of Psychology;" "Social Psychology."

Morgan: "Psychology of the Unadjusted School Child."

Mossman: "Teaching and Learning in the Elementary School."

Myers: "What Is Religious Education?"

Norsworthy and Whitley: "Psychology of Childhood."

Ogden: "The Meaning of Psychology."

O'Shea: "The Child: His Nature and His Needs."

Overstreet: "About Ourselves;" "Influencing Human Behavior."

(Note: Not all of these books are approved, but certain chapters are very suggestive.)

174

Perrin and Klein: "Psychology."

Pierce: "Understanding Our Children."

Sanger: "What Every Boy and Girl Should Know."

Sheridan: "Growth in Religion."

Skinner, Gast, and Skinner: "Readings in Educational Psychology." (An excellent handbook.)

Soares: "Religious Education."

Stewart: "A Study of Adolescent Development."

Thorndike: "Educational Psychology," three volumes; "Educational Psychology—Briefer Course."

Woodworth: "Dynamic Psychology;" "Psychology—A Study of Mental Life."

Thom: "Everyday Problems of the Everyday Child."

Vieth: "Objectives in Religious Education;" "Teaching for Christian Living."

Zachry: "Personality Adjustments of School Children."

DATE DUE